THE ONE WORK

A JOURNEY
TOWARDS THE SELF

by Anne Gage

LONDON
VINCENT STUART LTD

FIRST PUBLISHED IN 1961
BY VINCENT STUART PUBLISHERS LTD
45 LOWER BELGRAVE STREET LONDON SW1

MADE AND PRINTED
IN GREAT BRITAIN
BY ROBERT CUNNINGHAM AND SONS LTD
ALVA
CLACKMANNANSHIRE

To My Mother and Father

To traverse the path of life impetuously
To cross all lives as upon a wire
To pass over all abysses in song
Is possible only for the selfless spirit
(From *Fiery World*, Agni Yoga Society)

ILLUSTRATIONS

Part One

IN THE AUTUMN THE WIND BLOWS LEAF AFTER LEAF
to the ground until at last a tree stands naked, stark, waiting for the
new life of spring.

Perhaps it is the same with all processes.

Is there One in me, who like the tree, discards experience after
experience, search after search, life after life until at last we meet face
to face? Do I work or does It work or do we both work for the same
end – that meeting?

Nothing can be discarded until its purpose is fulfilled. No tree can
put forth green leaves until the dead ones are gone. Can I experience the
Resurrection before I have discarded the dead leaves, the outworn garments, the old wineskin of self?

If I have come from unity into the illusion of separateness, is there
no way back into unity through discarding of self and finding of Self?
In the end, for the thrifty-minded, nothing is lost because both are one,
the lower, the outer emanating from and returning to the higher, the
inner.

While I do not know this, I impede the Return. I am fallen, exiled,
asleep. I lie as dead upon the streets of Egypt.

'Rise and awake,' You say, 'and perform the Twelve Labours of
Hercules.'

'Rise and awake, that the waters of the sea may allow you to come
into the Promised Land.'

And I say, 'Where is the guarantee that this is truth? I cannot risk myself in such a venture. Why cast me into anguish and
misery when I am content as I am? How do I know I can trust
You?'

Can I trust the sun and the moon? In the day there is no moonlight
but I know the moon is there and at night there is no sun but I know
we will meet at dawn.

A poet has written:

> Chaque âme a sa mission sur terre
> Celle qui me revient est de me souvenir

I

Et c'est pourquoi je pars en guerre
à grand bruit et fracas – contre l'oubli.[1]

Who will explain to me the meaning of this poem? What is my soul's mission? When will I remember it? Why must I go to war and how do I overcome forgetfulness?

Years ago I read these words and only now I understand them. Who shall not understand them if he is obsessed with the question of who and what and why he is? Everyman stands somewhere along the path of self-discovery, whether he is Christian, Muslim, Jew, Hindu, Buddhist, Communist or simply man. Each has perpetually to choose and on the nature of his choice depends his progress towards or away from Himself.

It is as simple as that. I am alone in the desert and have to find my way by the stars and learn to protect myself against the heat of the day and the cold of the night.

I live in an age of extraordinary revelation and extraordinary violence. If I lie asleep, I am its victim. If I awake, I may learn how to restore the stolen fire to heaven. If I am to use fire, I must know what fire is and who I am, so that fire does not use me. Will I realize before it is too late that in denying God I am denying my Self?

If this is the time of the world's choice and the Lords of Flame wait, praying that we may rise one note in the scale of being, could I forget my promise to seek Them? Ancient I am, but still too young to remember more than fragments of my Divine Origin and these, scattered by the winds of other men's doubt, are memories only; yet enough for me to apprehend the Presence of One Who calls to me across the bridge of my becoming.

How much have I lost in the rituals of indifference since the world began? No wonder I am hungry. No wonder I secretly speak to angels and want to know and want to know. It is as if I once knew and have forgotten and I am obsessed with the memory of what it was like not to be ignorant and I feel guilty.

Now that we are passing from the time of pride into the time of fear, what will be my hope? What will prevent the toppling of the tower of Babel and who will give bread instead of stones to the starving? Will I realize in time that I am the Pharisee, and that as I am, I cannot enter the temple? Will I laugh when I see that I am the camel trying to pass through the eye of the needle?

If I do not ask these questions now I will not awake from the first death and will proceed towards the second. I am useless to the world

[1] From the Provencal of Philadelphia de Gerde.

2

and to myself because I do not understand the mystery of earth or water or fire or air.

What is there East or West that will overcome hatred, anger, greed and fear? Who will be my guide and hold fast to my hand as I pass through the world?

Theseus had the thread of Ariadne to guide him through the labyrinth. What have I got? Who is my Ariadne? Perseus slew the Gorgon with the help of a shield burnished to mirror-brightness. Where is my shield? Who is the Gorgon? Gabriel blows the trumpet for the resurrection of the dead. What is the trumpet? Who are the dead? Michael is the Dragon-slayer and the Archangel of the sun. What is the Dragon and where the sun? What is the sword that slays the Dragon? Where are the seven spheres and the five elements? What are the Grail, the Pearl of Great Price, the Treasure? Who are their guardians and who the hero who passes through fire and water to obtain them? Whose is the Mystic Marriage and whose the Virgin Birth? What is Earth and what is Heaven and where is the Kingdom and who the King?

All religious traditions, all myths East and West give one answer.

My Guide through the labyrinth is called the Presence, the Sacrificed One, Reality, God, the Lamb slain from the beginning of the World, the True, Inner, Higher Self. He is Experience, Friend, Guru, Tester, Father.

And who am I? I am at present the world; the fallen; the wanderer; the brother-slayer. But I can arise in myself and become the Other. I can become the redeemer of my fallen self, he who treads the path of the sun through the twelve houses to become the Solar Hero. The One Who walks with me as my guide I call That because He takes a thousand forms.

I am Theseus and He is Ariadne and the labyrinth is myself. Part of me is Perseus and part Medusa and one will have to slay the other. I am dead until I can hear Gabriel's trumpet and carry Michael's sword into battle against the Dragon. The seven spheres and five elements are within me. They are the levels and divisions of my being and the ladder up which I climb to Heaven. When the sun arises in me, the light of the stars will vanish and I will have freed myself from their power. I seek the Grail, the Pearl of Great Price, the Treasure and I will find them in the cave of my heart. When they are found, the Mystic Marriage and the Virgin Birth will take place. Then I and my Father are one; Samsara and Nirvana are one; Earth and Heaven are one; I am the Kingdom and I am the King. I AM.

*   *   *   *

3

What man exists except the Enlightened who is not looking for something; whether food, happiness, wealth, success, power, or truth in one form or another? Who is without desire? All searches lead ultimately to this one; all desires are progressively experienced and abandoned until there remains only the desire to be one with God. All work that is a longing and a discovery, a dying and a birth, an effort and a growth leads in this direction. Every child that is born symbolizes the mystery of the soul's rebirth and Resurrection; every man and woman who loves reflects the Mystic Marriage of soul and Spirit, man and God. How is it then that those who have been and are the custodians of truth, have distorted it out of all recognition and have lost the key?

Perhaps because understanding cannot come unless the soul cries out for it. Truth cannot be the monopoly of institutions but is the last resort of the individual man in a world of mass production and mass destruction. It is the only Treasure beyond price that he can seek out for himself, by himself, in himself, in a thousand questions leading to a thousand more, in secret and alone.

*　　*　　*　　*

This is an age of eclipse when the light is hidden and hard to find. Theseus stumbles in the labyrinth and loses the thread. The minotaur grows fat on the bodies of the sacrificed.

On every side are heard the voices:

'I am an atheist.'

'I believe but I don't understand.'

'Religion is rubbish.'

'I am not sure about anything.'

'I would like to believe in God, but not the Christian God.'

'I can get along on my own.'

Men turn to destroy the letter of religion because they cannot find its spirit. In the darkness there is no light.

They cannot see the light, but might it not exist?

Am I to join in the work of destruction? Shall I stay with these voices and die? Or shall I look for the light? Shall I be slain by the minotaur or shall I find the sword and slay it? Shall I find the way out of the labyrinth?

I will search.

Where should I turn for guidance?

I appeal to those who have gone before, who have shown the Way. At first I love them for the beauty of their work alone and for a depth in it that draws me to them magnetically. I do not understand but I love. Then as I gather the fragments of many pasts and piece them together and try to ponder the meaning of events in my own life, I begin to understand – first that there is something to be understood that will help me; and then what that 'something' is.

They are isolated when I begin. In China there is Lao-Tze[1] and Chuang-Tze.[2] There are the painters of the Sung dynasty and the fragments of T'ang. There are the paintings in the Caves of Tun-Huang and the sculptures of Lung-Men. Instinctively, I feel they express the destiny of man. In Persia there are the mystic poets, Rumi,[3] Attar,[4] and Hafiz[5]. In India there are the temple sculptures and the Upanishads and the Bhaghavad Gita. In Tibet, there is the Book of the Dead. In Egypt, there are the Gods and temples and in Greece the myths and the mysteries.[6] In Europe there are fairy-tales and a tradition of heresies.[7] There are the Alchemists[8] and many saints and poets without number. There are the Legend of the Holy Grail and Gothic Churches and there are Holy Mountains, as in the East.

I am drawn to them each in turn with a thirst for truth. I love them because they help me to continue my search. But they need a key. I must find the key. I must learn how to understand them. Meanwhile, I love and love and love them and fly to them from the dead philosophies of Europe and the churches of unwarmed stone.

I hold the thread of Ariadne. I have their help. I am not alone. I know I cling to them too much and to my life not enough but when I find the key, the balance will be redressed.

Oh quickly find the key for there is never much time for searchers, though patience is one of the things they have to learn on the way. How much time have I wasted? For so many years there was never time to do more than laugh or cry as the circumstances demanded and it was very hard to force myself to look over the wall. What might there be beyond? Orderly rows of vegetables or a gardener tying up peach trees and waiting? Or mountains perhaps to be climbed or a desert to cross? How do I learn to walk by the light of the moon in the daytime and the light of the sun at night? Is it all a dream and when shall I awake?

But if I dare to look closer and be honest for once – always remembering the virtues of the Chinese sages – I can see that during these years there were two constant desires – the one for truth, the other for what I called life. Often I have mistaken one for the other and eagerly gulped up experience hoping thereby to discover truth. But then in the midst of experience, clenched in its fist, truth was forgotten and I ran down

[1] The Tao Teh King. [2] Books. [3] The 'Mathnavi'.
[4] The 'Conference of the Birds' by Farid-ud-Din Attar. [5] 'The Divan'.
[6] Orphic and Eleusinian. [7] The Gnostic, the Manichaean, the Albigensian.
[8] Roger Bacon, John Dee, Nicolas Flamel, Gerbert of Auvergne (Pope Silvester II), among others.

5

avenues trying to remember and crying because again I had made the same mistake. Is there no other way?

At intervals, there was a pause and the voice, always repeated, 'What do you really desire?' Oh, I have answered carelessly a thousand times, not realizing Who was asking and have answered variously; to grow up, to be clever and pass exams, to be independent, happy, powerful. But, to a certain degree, I was each in turn and still the questioner insisted: 'What do you really want?' How was I to know it was You asking – You Who for so long have been my Enemy and are now my Friend. I might have answered differently. Instead, I see now, the answers I gave were limited, and experience that I longed for and questioned and grasped frittered away in my hands. Not all, of course, for then I would have learned nothing, and never come to recognize You. There were those that did not possess me; those through which I passed as a fire-walker treading on coals with the soles of his feet intact. Then I could say with detachment: this is anger that is trying to seize me, or jealousy or fear, or greed or hate. It became clear that experience broken down resolves itself into separate emotions. Often and often the same one recurs until it can be recognized in advance and an ambush laid before I am overpowered and slain by the usual reaction.

But there were others that rushed without warning – too swiftly for recognition – into my life and shook and shattered and toppled the carefully-erected façade of self. Then it was impossible for the ignorant to be detached and emotions followed each other like tidal waves, each one engulfing further the island of self. Then I cried out, 'Why do these things happen to me?' 'What have I done to deserve them? Why am I made to suffer?' And, of course, I blamed God. But then if God doesn't exist – just supposing He doesn't for the sake of the argument who is to blame? Might it not be myself? I wondered. Of You at that time, I knew nothing. How could I guess Your hand was at work, hurrying me along the path that leads to Your Gate?

How could I know that these experiences are all a re-membering of what I am since the world began? If I think I am whole, how can I recognize the act of collecting the fragments of being?

Dimly, however, I did perceive the patterns of repetition. Slowly, in very little things, I tried to avoid the trap. Some experiences became tests. Others were still a blind enduring; others were the beginning of revelation. All, I now see, are trials: I am on trial by the world and the world by me. Mankind is on trial by man and man by his brother. I am on trial by You and You by me; the lower by the Higher and the Higher by the lower; man by God and God by man. But these are all one trial and they take place within me, in the courtroom of consciousness. Who is the Judge and who the judged; who the prosecutor and who the defender? What is the verdict? – for death or for life? These questions I ask because they must be asked and I will have to find the answers. I am responsible for the verdict. I am the Judge and I am the judged.

But this is a slow realization, perceived in retrospect, part of a process ever becoming. The same experiences recur, but they are lived differently: the same problems arise but have new resolutions; the same phrases are read but have new meaning. Why was it not possible to act or see in this way before? I am a little freer and at the same time more bound because more aware of what binds. There are no sharp divisions, no sudden revelations. It is a gradual recognition of what has always been there.

So many have gone this way and left the milestones to mark the stages of awakening, so that he who walks shall not be overcome by despair and will be able to pass through doubt. Each one has said in turn, 'I am a Man that am come from the City of Destruction and am going to the Mt. Zion, and I was told by the Man that stands at the Gate, at the head of this way, that if I called here, you would show me excellent things, such as would be a help to me in my Journey.'[1]

Each one has at some time, like Blake, burst into tears at the words 'And when he was yet a great way off, his Father saw him,' because he realized that he was the Prodigal Son.

I, too, now rise between midnight and dawn to squeeze anguish onto paper. If You would come closer, Presence I love. If there was no division and I not reaching across abysses of longing. I try to clean my house but there are still unopened rooms. I am so conscious of not-loving. But I am weary and want to rest. I act clumsily and when I speak, words fall heavily, letter without spirit. People withdraw. All the time I know I stand in Your Way and long to be able to lift my body from Your Path, so that Your clear singing can reach the world. Teach me how to give love instead of words. That would be better. No pedagogy. Life. Then winter would warm and rain assuage pain and snow reveal treasure, and the rose bloom at midnight without thorns.

In childhood there is no answer but one question leads to another. There is the bigness too great for the body and the parents that are King and Queen of a far country. There is the feeling that I do not belong and will one day return to my home. There is the oak tree in the garden where the fairies live and which has its own life as I have mine. But no-one says to it as they do to me when I ask questions: 'Don't be a silly little girl.' Maybe it doesn't need to ask. Maybe the

[1] *Pilgrim's Progress.*

7

sun speaks to it and tells it how to grow up. When will I be able to fly to the sun? If only I were a man. Then I could be like the Knights of the Grail and do brave things and kill dragons and rescue beautiful ladies. I am each hero in turn from the mist-shrouded legends of Scandinavia to the silken tales of the Arabian Nights. Please let me stay in your world and not go back to mine where there is always the voice telling me not to do this or that, giving no reasons, shutting up my heart in a cardboard box. Sinbad, let me go with you, and Jason with you. Thor, let me help you outwit Loki and hold your thunder-hammer. Launcelot marry me and take me with you on your search. King Arthur let me sit at your Round Table and go with you in the boat with the three Queens when they take you away to the island across the sea. What is life worth if I cannot be in your company? You will see, I am strong enough to fight dragons or I will lull them to sleep with song so that you may creep up behind them unawares. I will climb up Rapunzel's hair into her tower and carry her away with me across the wilderness and I will spin rooms of flax into gold by morning. I will ride with Galahad and see the Grail, and rub Aladdin's lamp, and find the talking bird and the singing tree. I will wear Arabian shoes and carry a golden sword, and marry a King's son.

Memory of magic fades. School begins and there is too much to remember. Instead of being the hero, I try to be like him. But these are the heroes of history and I do not love them in the same way. They are not as close. They are warriors, not princes. Their goal is power not truth. There are Hannibal and Ghenghiz Khan, Caesar and Agamemnon, Alexander and Cortez. In the beginning school is exciting. Teachers are Gods, opening avenues, offering knowledge. Marvelling, I imagine the splendour of Montezuma's gold. Civilizations rise and fall; some buried by sand; some lost in dark jungles, awaiting discovery. There are the adventurers, in search of new worlds; Columbus and Ponce de Leon whose name is a song. He sailed from Spain to find the Fountain of Eternal Youth. It was in the East. But he went West by mistake and came to Florida and died there of fever. I learn all this by heart and try to please and am very clever but I am not happy and do not understand.

It is the end of the war but in the little world of school there is battle and the cries of children sworn to enmity. Competition, ridiculing the weak, mocking of difference; violence, despising of gentleness; shivering with cold and shivering with fear. It is clear that I am neither as clever as Sinbad nor as lucky as Aladdin. But there is the fascination of learning – Shakespeare and the law of the jungle. And a new love is growing, a love of sounds in poetry; a love of mathematics where there

8

is always the right solution to a problem, black marks on white paper, precise, within reach of my comprehension.

For the rest the questions are not answered. 'Why do civilizations vanish? When was the real dawn of history? What is the origin of the world, of man, of me? Why am I here, going to this school, born of these parents, the person I am?'

Only in literature is there some sort of answer for at least the questions come from the heart, asked by someone who felt the same way. Only in poetry can I forget the pain of undigested facts and the fear of failing to remember enough. History I like because there are a few men who are interesting. Science is to be mastered if I wish to succeed. But there is no room for wonder; they do not last beyond the moment. They are no more than a series of facts to be memorized for a series of exams. They feed my curiosity but not my longing to know.

'What is war?' I ask. 'Why does it happen?' Can history answer me, or science? Poetry says: 'It is the nightmare within the sleep.' 'But why doesn't God stop the war?' I ask because I have learned that God is responsible for everything. Science does not recognize God and history tells me that He has not stopped war in the past. Poetry says 'Why should He stop what man has started?' 'God must be on our side,' I say, to comfort myself. 'He can't want good people to be killed.' But another part of me asks why. 'Because the parson said so last Sunday. He said we were right and therefore God would help us to win.' But that is not an answer. That is what I have heard but I am not sure. Supposing the parsons in Germany say the Germans are right and God will help them. Can He help both at once? Why should He help either? Maybe He is punishing us for sins committed hundreds or thousands of years ago. Maybe we are paying our debts. Doesn't the Bible say it is wrong to kill? Why do men kill?

If neither teacher, nor church, nor parent can give me an answer, where else shall I look?

To my dreams perhaps?

There is the dream of the country I shall always return to after the war is over; the country that is always over the north pole, beyond the land of the Hyperboreans. Yet it has the smell of the earth – the sun smell and the pine smell coming up from the valley on the wings of the wind, and the roses and dry grass. Yes, and the tall black cypresses and the olive trees that dance down to the sea and above all, the mountain. The mountain is an Angel with red wings, guarding the valley. No-one may enter who does not belong because the Angel will not let him pass the gate.

There is the dream of the swan. I stand in a garden between two

9

cypresses and the roses are as big as moons and I am very small. One tree speaks to me: 'Have you come, child, to begin your quest?' 'Yes,' I answer because that is the truth. 'Then enter,' the other says to me. And I am on the other side. Before me stretches an endless sea of blue, as clear and still as glass. There is no living thing to be seen. Far away, beyond the horizon, I see a white speck. Nearer it comes. A thousand years pass before I see that it is a swan. It has a purple cloak on its back and a golden crown on its head and is three times as big as I am. I stand there and cry because it is so beautiful. It speaks to me and I hear it saying, 'Come, child, mount.' I wonder how I will ever climb onto its back, but suddenly I am there with my arm around its neck and my legs in front of its left wing. The warmth of its body comforts me. We rise higher and higher into the sky until I can see the earth no longer. 'Where do you fly, Swan?' I ask it.

'Towards Infinity.'

'What is Infinity?'

'That which is.'

'I cannot understand.'

'Stay with Me and I will bring you to it.'

'How can I stay with you?'

'Remember my words and choose the right-hand path.'

'Who are You?'

'A part of yourself.'

'And who am I?'

'A child of earth and Starry Heaven.'

He returns me to earth but not before He has shown me all the countries of the world and all the stars in heaven.

'I will not forget,' I cry, 'I will not forget. I am a child of earth and Starry Heaven, of earth and Starry Heaven.'

But I forget because this is a dream and I cannot bring it together with my waking life, and my waking life is drawing me to it more and more so that I am in the middle of a whirlpool and cannot get out. There is no time. There are lessons to be learned and games to be played and friendships to be made. There are the loves to be loved and the hates to be hated and the fears to be overcome. There is the cleverness in school and the clumsiness at home because one is easy to grasp and the other is not. There are people, more and more people entering my life. Each one is new, different, nice or nasty. My body is growing but is still too small. I have mountains of joy and valleys of despair to travel across every day. There is no time to remember. My knowledge is dust in my mouth. I may learn everything by heart and pass exams brilliantly, but inside I am dying of hunger and thirst. I cannot ride any longer with a lance in my hand across the flat golden plain and feel the wind blowing through my hair.

One day there is an experience that shocks me into memory of You, Swan. It is not a dream because it happens when I am awake. It is not dying because I am still alive. I see the colour blue all round me. I feel the bed sliced beneath me as by a knife and I am pushed into the crevice. I try to open my mouth to call for help, but no words come. I try to open my eyes but my eyelids are weighted like stone. A buzzing and roaring like an avalanche deafens and terrifies me. I enter a small tube – large enough for thought only. I emerge from it and from the tumult of my passage into silent space and rest there, attached to my body by a fine cord. Waiting there for what will happen, I hear a voice that says, 'I AM.' Then fear seizes me and I am forced back into the channel, back into my body. Astonished I open my eyes with ease, hear my voice, am aware of my arms and legs.

The experience never comes again. But it is enough to stir me to action. I have discovered something I did not know existed. What is within? Whose is the voice that says, 'I AM'? What does it mean, that phrase? What am I? I will not rest until I know. I am twelve; old enough to begin my search. Who will answer my questions?

Start with what is near at hand. When I go to church on Sundays, with the other children, it is an unpleasant duty. Nausea and faintness assail me. The words repeated each week are memorized but spoken only with the lips. Words are intoned without joy or love to us who do not understand but are oppressed by the weight of sin placed upon our hearts. I feign illness on Sundays. When there is no escape, hatred leaves me like a tree without sap.

But I will ask questions and weigh the answers.

What are the things we have done that we ought not to have done and the things we have left undone that we ought to have done? Why is there no health in us? What are the ways that we have strayed from? What are our manifold sins and wickedness? What are God's Holy Laws? Why are we miserable offenders?

I am told that I am a sinner. But what have I done? Do I bear the burden of the whole human race? I am told that God is all around us, that He sees what we do and hears our prayers but what is He: a man, an Angel, or something like the air I breathe? Can the sacrifice of Christ redeem me? Why do I need to be redeemed? If Christ really redeemed mankind, why is there suffering?

I am told about the Fall but where have I fallen from, and why?

I ask about heaven and am told I will go there when I die but I am not sure that I want to go.

11

Hell is a place where bad people go but how does God know who is really bad?

I want to know why I am alive; what the purpose of life is but the church does not give me an answer I can understand.

I refuse to be confirmed until I know what God is and what I am.

Someone tells me about Boehme, a mystic who lived in Germany in the sixteenth century. I begin to read his *Way to Christ*[1] and there I find much that puzzles and interests me, and that, for the first time, expresses exactly what I have felt.

'Alas,' he says, 'the faith of this day is but historical – no more than assent to the matter of fact that Jesus Christ lived and died, that the Jews killed Him, that He left this world, and is not King on earth in the outward man, but that men may do as they list and need not die from sin.'

But this is not his interpretation of Christianity.

'It appeareth that it is not so easy a matter to be a Christian and that Christianity doth not consist in the mere knowing of the history and applying the knowledge thereof to ourselves, saying that "Christ died for us, and hath destroyed death and turned it into life in us, and He hath paid the ransom for us so that we need do nothing but comfort ourselves therewith and steadfastly believe that it is so."

'A Christian should therefore consider why he calleth himself a Christian and examine truly whether he be one or not. For surely by learning to know and confess that I am a sinner and that Christ hath destroyed my sins on the cross and shed His blood for me, doth not make me a Christian.

'A Christian is of no sect. He can dwell in the midst of sects and appear in their services without being attached or bound to any. He hath but one knowledge, and that is, Christ in him. . . . He wisheth continually that the truth of God might be done in him and that His Kingdom might be manifested in him.'

Does this mean that Christ is within me; that I need not go to church in order to be close to Him?

'Men,' he continues, 'tie us in these days to the history and to the material churches of stone; which churches are good in their kind, if men did also bring the temple of Christ into them. They teach moreover that their absolution is a forgiving of sins and that the supper of the Lord taketh away sin; Also that the Spirit of God cometh into men through their ministry. All which hath a proper meaning, if it were rightly understood; and if men did not cleave merely to the husk.'

What *is* the proper meaning? I wonder.

[1] (Watkins).

12

'Many a man goeth to church twenty or thirty years, heareth sermons, receiveth the Sacraments and heareth absolution read, and yet is as much a beast of the devil and vanity at the last as at the first. A beast goeth into the church and to the Supper and a beast cometh out from thence again.'

'What good end doth it answer for me to go to the material churches of stone, and there fill my ears with empty breath? Or to go to the Supper and feed nothing but the earthly mouth? Cannot I satisfy that with a piece of bread at home? What good doth it to the soul, which is an immortal life, to have the bestial man observe the form and venerate the shell of Christ's institution, if it cannot obtain the kernel thereof?'

Dimly I perceive that here is someone who has found the answer; who knows the truth.

'And thus,' he says, 'with absolution also. What benefit is it to me for one to say, "I pronounce and declare to thee the forgivenss of thy sins" when my soul is wholly shut up in sin? Whoever saith thus to a sinner so shut up erreth; . . . None can forgive sins but God only. . . . The preacher hath no forgiveness of sins in his own power; but it is the spirit of Christ in the voice of the priest that hath the power, provided the priest himself is a Christian.

'The Sacraments do not take away sin; neither are sins forgiven thereby. But it is thus: When Christ ariseth, then Adam dieth in the essence of the serpent; as when the sun riseth the night is swallowed up in the day and the night is no more.'

Does this mean that all is within me? Is God in me? Is Adam myself and how can he die? What can make Christ rise in me?

'All such flattery of ourselves by saying, "Christ hath paid our ransom and made satisfaction for sin" and that "He died for our sins" if we also do not die from sin in Him . . . is a false and vain comfort.

'Therefore it is not so easy a matter to become a child of God as men imagine.

'A man must wrestle till the dark centre, that is shut up close, break open and the spark lying therein kindle and from thence immediately the noble lily-branch sprouteth as from the divine grain of mustard-seed, as Christ saith.

'He must for a while become a fool in his own reason . . . until Christ be formed in this new incarnation. And then when Christ is born, Herod is ready to kill the Child, which he seeketh to do outwardly by persecutions and inwardly by temptations.'

Can Christ then be eternally reborn in man? How can this come about?

He says: 'Light and darkness are both in him (man) but each of them dwelleth in itself and neither possesseth the other; but if one of them entereth into the other and will possess it, then that other loseth its power.

'The eternal darkness of the soul is hell which is called the anger of God, but the eternal light in the soul is the Kingdom of Heaven.

'But if heaven in man be not open and the man stand without heaven flattering himself and say, "I am still without but Christ will take me in through His Grace; is not His merit mine?" such a one is in vanity and sin with the outward man and with the soul in hell, in the anger of God.'

What must happen for the light to overpower the darkness?

'War assaulteth the whole man. The outward fleshly man fighteth against the inward spiritual man and the spiritual against the fleshly and so man is in continual warfare and strife, full of trouble, misery, anguish and care.

'The inward Spirit saith to the fiery soul, "O my soul! O my love! Turn I beseech thee and go forth from vanity or else thou loseth thy love and the noble Pearl."

'Then saith the outward reason (the bestial soul), "Thou art foolish; wilt thou be a laughing stock and the scorn of the world? Thou needst the outer world to maintain this life. Beauty, power and glory are thy proper happiness; wherein only thou canst rejoice and take delight. Why wilt thou cast thyself into anguish, misery and reproach? Take thy pleasure which will do both thy flesh and thy mind good." '

So there is One in me Who desires that I should come to Him, Who awaits release. I am not only the person I am used to living with. There is more to me than that. In me perhaps are God and Christ and all the Angels but how do I reach Them?

'All Christian religion,' he says, 'wholly consisteth in this, to learn to know ourselves; whence we are come and what we are.'

Was this what the Greeks meant by 'Know Thyself'?

I turn then to books that speak about the mystery of life; books on occultism, theosophy.[1]

These teach me that there are great mysteries to be fathomed and that it is possible for man to do so; that there exists a destiny for man far beyond the establishment of peace or a material Utopia or a mythical life after death; that man's purpose on earth is to discover that destiny and that if he truly desires to know it, he will be taught step by step. They say that in his hands alone rests the possibility of his growth and development. If he wishes to change the future, he must act differently in the present. Long ages have passed before the desire is born in him

[1] *The Secret Doctrine*, Blavatsky (Theosophical Publishing House, Adyar).

to want to live differently and to know the truth. Long ages may pass before he learns how to co-operate intelligently with what are called the Higher Beings, or the 'hidden' part of himself. In the case of all men, what is experienced now is the result of what has been done in past lives and what is done now determines what will happen in the future. In this sense all men are equal because all have the possibility of spiritual growth. Revelation is the result of aspiration and aspiration is the love of what is higher than oneself.

Yes, this makes more sense to me, but how do I begin? How do I sort out the mass of thoughts and emotions which I am, and bring them into line with the desire to grow spiritually? Where do I start? There are the Greek ideals: Truth, Beauty, Goodness, Justice. But they are remote, like the Seven Wonders of the Ancient World. The Greeks had time to be philosophers, but I have to go to school every day. When I am reading, I am one-pointed, ordered, intensely happy. But when I am living everything is confusion. I am a piece of cloth torn by many hands. At school I am what I am asked to be, a clever pupil. At home I am the difficult child. I speak as I please, hurt when I can, spread my depression far and wide, furiously resent criticism, the admonishment to develop self-control. Why am I so good when I am learning, reading, so bad when I am not? I pray to be nicer for a few days but the habit of prayer vanishes and I am worse than ever. I demand love and make scenes of anger, resentment, jealousy, self-pity. I am locked in deadly combat with my brother. I am lost in the labyrinth. Where is Ariadne's thread? Why can't I get out? After all, I've read about the Higher Beings. Why don't they help me? If They won't do their part, I can't do mine. Its all too much of an effort; too far away. I have an exam coming up. There isn't time to lead both lives.

I turn my back upon You although You are still unknown to me. I cannot really hear Your voice although I can guess what You are saying. 'Your problem is pride. Your lesson humility. You have many a friend on the other side but you will not accept their help. You are afraid of them. You are wrong in believing that dedication means confusion. It is possible to tread this earth firmly without losing contact with the inner forces that condition life.'

Time and again I hear these words and still the pendulum swings back and forth between indifference and longing to be different and I am out of balance.

Once in a while an effort is made. Very slowly I see the hurt I give when I speak cruelly with my clever tongue; I become aware that distress is greater after anger than before; that jealousy makes me feel sick; that self-pity is no way out.

Hope, a tiny hope that it might be possible to escape from the prison of what I am, grows. Then I try too hard. I pray too often and become tense with the effort to control. My will snaps and everything is worse than before.

Then again, Your voice comes in the pages of a book I open one day. 'Do not try so hard to be good. Think of the flowers and how they grow in beauty. They don't try to be good. They merely turn their faces towards the sun for its warmth and healing rays and allow the beauty with which God has endowed all his children to develop naturally. Let joy enter your heart.'

But joy will not enter. Angrily I say that I cannot expand like a flower.

'Beware of tension and impatience,' You say. 'Learn to endure smilingly and to wait.'

But there is so much to be done. I want to reach the goal.

Again and again You warn me:

Beware of greed; impatience: advance one step at a time.

It may be that my mother or father speaks to me, or a page of a book, or a word of a poem. I do not yet recognize You speaking through them but I listen because there is comfort and help. The years pass and I search. There are moments of finding, moments of deeper experience. Two weeks condition a whole year.

There is a journey to Spain in spring when terraces built by the Moors are white with almond blossom. South is the Alhambra, archetype of palaces; rosy stone and alabaster; courtyards to wander in, lions and fountains; a garden to contain love. At Cordoba, besides the mosque, there were nine miles of palaces, and at night the road was open to travellers seeking wisdom. Many came from the East to live there and fragments of their knowledge, sifting northwards, reached Paris in translation. When destruction came, a few who knew, fleeing Christian swords, went northwards, over mountains, secretly, to pass on the Cup of Truth to other hands, more Christian.

I flee the churches of the North, unholy, decaying, not yet purified of inquisitors' guilt. And cities still twisted by torture; Salamanca, Saragossa. Cold unpitying stone; cold unpitying man, driving to death, life.

Roncesvalles at dusk gives no sound of Roland's horn. Only the spirit of Charlemagne looks north and south, guarding the pass for the traveller.

I discover that places move me to write and writing helps me to see. The meaning is clear years later but I follow the thread of love. I long to travel so that I may love what I discover. It is a way out of the labyrinth.

While I am at Oxford, acquiring more knowledge, preparing for yet another exam, answering always questions like 'With what success did the English in the sixteenth century attempt to reach the East by a northern passage?' instead of the inner ones, there are journeys, south to the light. There the fire of the mind dies for a while and the fire of the heart can burn. There I meet St. Francis in the paintings of his contemporaries, and the great red Angel who hovers in the Umbrian skies. In Siena and all the towns of Tuscany and Umbria I see the work of men to whom the air itself is revelation, to whom rock and earth and sky and man and angel are one. I feel that painting as a praising, a loving, a longing is communication with and a method of discovering God.

There is a service in the Lower Church at Assisi with walls and ceilings blue as the dome of heaven and a green carpet up to the altar and the Papal chair empty like the siege perilous of Arthur's table; and tall tapers to show the way. It is a Requiem for the Dead. I listen to the strange Latin words, translating here and there:

'May the angels receive thee in Paradise . . . and bring thee into the Holy City, Jerusalem . . . deliver the souls from the pains of hell . . . save them from the mouth of the lion . . . nor allow the dark lake to swallow them up . . . Lamb of God who takest away the sins of the world, give them eternal rest and let perpetual light shine upon them.'

And suddenly I realize that the words are addressed not to the dead but to us the living, the congregation of the world who have not awoken from our sleep and tears runnel my face as I listen to the voice of a boy that is like the singing of an Angel, and full of joy.

In Siena, head tilted backwards, I become the warrior, Guidoriccio da Fogliano and I set out for the battlefield, armed as for war.

At Borgo San Sepolcro I gaze at the image of what I may become. I worship the Essence of what I am. I, too, will arise and overcome death. You have shown the Way. I will follow.

I stand before Greek temples in Sicily and see them at first historically, then as art and architecture, then as symbols and finally I take them into me, and let their golden columns warm and lighten my house.

I know it now and can put it into words but then I was only conscious of a tremendous emotion and a love of men who had made something marvellous. Understanding came at first as communication, then as love, then as a gradual translation into my own time and space of what belongs to all times and places and is eternal, indivisible and holy.

I go to the strong, apocolyptic wilderness where a saint[1] lives,

[1] Padre Pio.

17

almost suffocated by pilgrims. I climb the hill on a starlit morning to attend mass and receive his blessing. There is a scent of violets but I can experience nothing in the multitude. I decide to return to Rome but the taxi-driver will not let me leave before I have been to the shrine of the Archangel.[1] He is my guide. With one eye on the road and the other over his shoulder, he tells me the story of the shrine as, still in the hour before dawn, we drive towards it. St. Michael forms in my mind. I am again the pilgrim, collecting a fragment of the past.

I am led into a whitewashed church. My driver holds his cap in his gnarled hands; down a flight of broad stone steps. We are Crusaders descending into the bowels of the earth, pilgrims to the Holy Land, seeking the blessing of the Guardian. At the bottom there is the cave and over the entrance the words: 'This is the abode of God, the Gateway to Heaven.' Does God dwell in a cave and why is it the gateway to heaven? We hesitate and my companion speaks: 'Yes, it is a holy place, often I feel the Archangel is here, but you must not be afraid to enter. You would not have come if it were not His Will.'

I go in. On my right is an altar and inscribed on it the words spoken by St. Francis when he came here in the thirteenth century. 'Lord,' I read, 'I am not worthy to enter Thy House.' Has he, too, been here then, whom I have loved since I was twelve? Was it the Archangel, Face of the Presence and Friend of man who appeared to him on Mt. Laverna? He who is Captain of the Hosts of the Lord, had He helped him with his inner struggle? Will He help me with mine? St. Francis had gone no further. Should I?

'Come,' said my guide, 'have no fear.' So I follow him into the heart of the mountain and stand among the glistening, black, furrowed walls. I look round me for the Archangel and see only chairs in front of an altar and an old woman monotonously sweeping the floor. I go forward and kneel on one of the chairs before the altar and lay my head upon my arms and let darkness overtake my mind and surrender myself to what happens. I wait. A reservoir burst somewhere within; tears flow; tears that are the defence of the soul against the inrushing of Spirit, that prevent it from burning in the fire of experience. They are the offering of myself to Him. They are the only means I have of expressing the longing to give and the longing to receive. They are the unity of my whole being, crying for release from the prison of ignorance and darkness and suffering. For a few moments, I realize that in asking for help for myself, I ask for the whole world and feel the weight of its sorrow and hear its cry of despair. And because I feel and hear, so I know the

[1] Monte Gargano, or Monte Sant' Angelo.

18

Archangel feels and hears and will give answer for He is the Wielder of the Sword that cuts the bonds of ignorance and slays the Mighty Dragon.

There are periods of doubt – months, even years when I turn my back upon wanting to know and get on with living everyday life. Then what I have learned is dismissed as the welling up of personal feeling, neither true nor false, of little use to me or anyone else. I lose the one and am lost in the many. Doubt is my companion. But with doubt comes a sense of the worthlessness of life. There is nothing to hang onto except a sequence of events without meaning. Life is a wilderness and I pass through it without food or water. In this state I crouch in the shadows of cities that are like jungles; ruthless, brutal, terrifying. I am separated from people by abysses of ignorance and fear. I am one of millions who live in uniform and spend their lives in sacrifice to the Idols of War, Peace, Prosperity, Progress, Success, Security. I am aware that the advance of our knowledge has put an end neither to hatred nor fear. The old problems are not solved and new ones appear daily. The memory of outrageous suffering is fading but the fear of outrageous suffering is growing. This is the labyrinth and where is Ariadne's thread?

I turn to religions as they are today and find division instead of unity; many opinions but no knowledge of truth.

I turn to science in great wonder of what can be achieved for man-kind but I tremble that knowledge without compassion will bring destruction.

I turn to the pursuit of success in the hope that here I may forget the need to know the truth.

I strike back in fury at all institutions that suffocate – religion, law, convention, thereby increasing the sum of distress.

I give up and don't get out of bed in the morning.

I turn my face to the wall and cry out that there is no God, no purpose to existence; no way, no truth, no mystery, no light.

But if I accept none of these, I have to accept the fact of my own body, my own being. If I do not kill myself I am alive.

So it is one night when despair has overpowered me and I lie in darkness, writhing as the images of my life pass before me and strengthen the feeling that I can go no further and want to die.

But in the exhausted silence after tears, I hear a voice, so clearly that I sit up and listen.

'Of what use is it to cry, child, and to weep with midnight loneliness when all the world is dying and the thunder of the Great Ones trembles the night air?'

Of what use is it to cry? I ask myself. The voice is right. How long have I been asleep? And I realize that three years have passed and I am twenty-four. I want to live. Energy courses through me and the need to discover.

What am I? I write, black words on white paper. An answer is within.

'You are a woman; young, ignorant, sorrowful, searching and separate: thinking too much, loving, laughing at times. You are of the West, the moon-apparelled world; a child of cities where rhythm is muffled by noise, where beauty is not upon faces and fear walks.

'You have been taught to think along rigid lines, without feeling except where poetry has brought tears. You are cognizant of philosophical systems, theories, a multitude of facts, and Ignorance.

'Your life consists of resistance to what comes, reactions to what you like or dislike; gossip; patterns of lying; futility. You have forgotten the Lion-hearted.'

What should I do? What should I do?

If I could tune in my longing to the creativeness of space, then would words write, joy flow, pain know, fear cease and sound reverberate. Then could I weep myself into ecstasy knowing the usefulness of suffering. Then would all journeys into pasts made splendid by recollection, into futures pinnacled with hope be undertaken without striving and despair be welcomed as a prelude to understanding.

But this experience is not yet.

How to know it?

I want to write and have nothing to say. I want to answer other people's questions and cannot answer my own. Who will clarify what is obscure?

I look back over the past twelve years, at the searches pursued and the knowledge accumulated and I look at my life as it is – a tangled mass of relationships with people I do not love but to whom I am bound by desire and ambition and fear of loneliness and habit.

I still do not understand more than that there is something to be understood.

Must I then return back the way I have come, since it has led me nowhere, trying to find the first mistake? Past all the unlearning achieved by learning and the Babylonian towers of other people's knowledge? I am imprisoned by my own inadequacy. What gestures of compassion can I make? What can I say to those lost in the labyrinth like myself – the angry, the proud, the fearful, the pitiless, the despairing; and to those who cry out: 'How can I bear the torment of this senseless undirected struggle?' All are me and I am all. Love is very far away. What I call love is really a grabbing of bread to satisfy my hunger, of comfort so that I may forget my fear. No giving, for what have I to give? What I extort from others in the name of love saying: 'I must have this, you must love me so,' dies soon. I demand it on my own terms and it cheats me. I lie alone though one lies with me. I am neither wise nor loving but as the labourer who knew how to sow but forgot to put in the living seed, so that when summer comes, his fields are barren and he suffers the pangs of hunger.

How can I break this pattern of dying? How find someone to help me?

I will arise and go unto my Father. My money is spent and I am weary of this life.

I am of the West. I will go East, I will go away to come back, break the pattern of my life, stretch my soul.

Voices protest.

'What are you running away from?'

'I suppose you're going in search of your soul!'

'You'd better get married and forget all this nonsense.'

'Life has no purpose so why not get on with living it.'

'Idealists always come to grief.'

Shut up! I say to them.

To be Lion-hearted, one must walk towards fire.

They are silent and in the great new strength that I feel I write:

'December . . . is the birth month, when what is hidden gestates. There is preparation for the Coming-Forth. It is the death month when what can be relinquished dies, making possible the next phase. It is therefore the time to inaugurate journeys and to cast off the bands that pinion the wings of the Swan.'

How long ago did I forget the Swan?

December is always the birth month and the time of passing the Guardian at the Gate of Death, the struggle with Cerberus and the return. Do I not pass the Gate a thousand times before I enter the Kingdom?

I will go East because East is the part of me I do not know. I am the shore and it is the ocean and I stand at its edge and wonder what lies in its depths.

And the East in the outer world is India because India is the symbol of truth to be discovered. India is the destination of all explorers; the Pearl of great price, the Fountain of Eternal Youth; the unknown, mysterious, fabulous land.

India is hardly more than a fragrance. As when a child I believed in fairy-tales and the memory of that world of legend lingered as I grew into life, so now I believe in India. It is to me as was Prester John to the early explorers – a key to far-off worlds.

Now it seems as if each line of poetry that has stirred the reeds of longing; each image of beauty and fragment of what seemed to be truth, has served to uncover, layer by layer, a decision that I have taken centuries ago. Nothing is wasted. I have had to search and wander for twelve years and maybe twelve thousand in all the varied experience of life, through all that has come to me before I can realize its presence.

The decision to go to India is therefore no sudden choice made after a night of questioning. It has always been with me, awaiting the moment of recognition.

Part Two

AS IF EVERYTHING HAD BEEN PLANNED IN ADVANCE, the means of reaching India appeared. I had three weeks to prepare; three weeks in which to enter unknown rooms in the house of the world, to imagine the unimaginable.

I began to read about Asia; exercising intellect and memory. Books filled my table and floor, maps my walls. I pored over them trying to fix in my mind the peninsulas and irregular coastlines and strange-sounding names. I came across words of a poem that express the wonder of discovery.

> Suddenly, in new splendour
> Secretly
> In golden smoke there gleamed
> Swiftly awakened in the steps of the sun
> Fragrant with a thousand peaks
> Asia appeared to me,
> And blinded, I sought one that I knew. . . .[1]

Never had I thought of it as a part of my world. I could not imagine its people, its civilizations, its problems. No further than Persia had I wandered in curiosity. Hong Kong was a name as fabulous as Timbuktu. Japan was associated with the war and the prints that hang on the walls of western houses; Malaya with rubber; Siam with a New York musical; Burma with the prisoners who died there; India with Gandhi and Clive and Warren Hastings.

Now I read about Ajanta and the thousands of temples in India, the poverty and the sacred cows. And about Angkor – the city hidden in the jungles of Cambodia; about Indonesia and its struggle for independence. I tried to grasp the stupendous contribution of China and the vitality of Japan. Beneath this ignorance of the outer Asia there lurked the apprehension that it promised a richer experience than any I had known and that the shock of my contact with it would re-orientate my life; raise me above the level of the plain so that I could survey the valley

---

[1] Hoelderlin.

23

and the flow of the river from a higher vantage point; go beyond my limitations; understand a little more.

The journey, like all intensely lived journeys, breathed with its own rhythm and I breathed with it. There was no time for fear. I was the experience and full of love. Each moment was new, requiring instant-aneous adjustment of mind and senses; Cyprus, Bahrein, Karachi, Calcutta: the flight towards the sun. The heart beat more rapidly – I was about to set foot in new worlds. To my left was the white blaze of the Himalaya. To my right the vastness of India. And below me the East: merchants fingering silks, jewellery from Tibet brought over the high passes, curved shoes, the smell of incense and stale perfume. I entwined myself in the first saree and laughed for joy. It was night as we flew over Burma. The lights of Rangoon were jewels in the coffers of a Prince.

Bangkok was the first destination. India had to be approached with patience. The great 'plane warmed up its engines one by one. The pilot waved as it turned into the runway. It rose like a swan into the hazy, heavy sky.

The drive into Bangkok took an hour. I sat in the car and looked out of the open window, perspiring in the steamy heat. All along the road were two slimy green canals and little wooden houses raised slightly above them on piles. I could look into them as I passed, as into a Flemish interior, and see the families preparing and eating their breakfast – each group separate and intact. Children shuffled in the hot recesses or splashed in the canals. The road itself was crowded with people going to work and waiting for the noisy white buses to take them into the city. The women wore white blouses and blue or black skirts – a kind of uniform. The men wore white shirts and trousers and looked im-maculate. They waited at the bus stops with no trace of impatience. For colour in this landscape there was only the grey road, the grey-green water, the darker buffalo wallowing there, the leaden sky. Occasionally there was the orange flash of a monk's robe. This was an East I did not expect.

Nor was life in Bangkok what I had expected.

I explored Bangkok in the small trishaws that were able to weave in and out of the crowded streets more easily than cars. It was a sprawling city of shacks and modern concrete buildings. There was a strong American influence everywhere. The people, too, seemed modern, without the burden of ancientness.

All the colour in Bangkok was concentrated in the temples. They rose gay and gaudy above the grey-brownness of the city, coated with plaster and heavily gilded. Inside they were dimly lit and stuffy with incense and lack of air. Tapers lit the gold of statues that crowded their halls, and the paintings that covered their high walls. The temples were my first contact with Buddhism. It seemed a friendly unfrightening religion. People came and went, said their prayers, ate their meals, chattered to their children, all in front of the many images of the Buddha. There seemed to be an element of propitiation in their offerings, as if Buddhism had been superimposed on something far older.

I wanted to know more about it, and so, one evening, hearing the story of an image of the Buddha that had been brought from one of the temples outside Bangkok into another temple in the city itself, I decided to go and see it. A few weeks before, a monk had by accident chipped off a piece of the plaster that had covered it, and had seen beneath it a gleam of gold. The rest had been hurriedly removed and the statue revealed in its full splendour. It had been brought in triumph into the city, and people were making pilgrimages from miles around to see it.

I joined the queue which started far outside the temple walls and wended my way slowly into the whitewashed room where it was – a huge seated statue, reaching from floor to ceiling, completely extraordinary. I knelt in prayer with the others.

After dinner that evening, a Thai woman answered some of my questions.

'Why is it so different from most of the other images?' I asked her.

'For a statue of the Buddha to have been made in gold and in that size, it must have been made by people who knew, and as it was valued very highly because of its effect on the people who prayed before it for guidance and inspiration, it was covered with plaster at the time of the Burmese invasions, so that it would not be stolen. No-one gave away the secret.'

'What do you mean by the words "people who knew"?'

'We use that term when we speak of those who are closer than we to an understanding of the mystery of life – who are nearer to Nirvana than we are.'

After that, whenever an opportunity occurred, I asked where I could learn more about Buddhism. I was no longer afraid to appear ridiculous, and although I was often given evasive answers, my interest was noted and the word got around. So it happened, that one night, when I asked someone where I could contact a teacher of meditation, I was at last given an answer.

'I will send you to my own. I see that you are really interested.'

'Tomorrow?'

'Yes, if you wish.'

An interpreter arrived to take me to the temple. I entered a huge quadrangle, surrounded by a high whitewashed wall and rows of cubicles divided by curtains, where, I supposed, the monks slept. It was spotlessly clean. In the centre were two buildings with a large patch of grass between them. Four or five groups of monks and their disciples were sitting there, talking quietly.

The interpreter took me over to one of these groups and presented me to the monk who seemed to be teaching, saying that I was a friend of Madame —— and that I wanted to learn the method of meditation that he had been teaching her.

I had never done any meditation before and didn't know what it meant other than sitting still and trying to concentrate.

'You have done meditation before?' the monk asked me through the interpreter.

'No.'

He smiled. 'Then I will show you an exercise.' He pointed to his pupils who had spread out a long rattan mat and were pacing its twenty feet, lifting their legs as if heavy weights were attached to them and setting them down slowly.

'The object of this exercise,' he explained, 'is to become more aware of each movement and effort of will that we make.'

Feeling foolish and not understanding the meaning of what he said, because the idea was so new to me, I took off my shoes and began to copy the others. At first embarrassment interfered with concentration, but as I lifted one foot after the other with infinite slowness, I became aware of how many decisions go into the making of one tiny movement. I had never thought in this way before and saw a vista of possibilities. If this applies to physical movements, then how much more so to thought and emotion. How aware was I of my mental and physical reactions?

I was not the only one to find the exercise interesting. All over the quadrangle men and women were walking as if through water, their attention focused upon sensing their legs and feet as they lifted and stepped and turned.

I left the temple exhilarated.

Hardly had I returned when the telephone rang. It was my friend. Her voice was excited.

'You went to the Meditation Hall! You went!'

'Why, yes. It was terribly interesting.'

'I hear all about it from the interpreter. Now you must go to a temple outside the city where there is a wonderful teacher. I will send a car for you tomorrow morning.'

26

'But I am leaving tomorrow.'

'Never mind. You go early. You must go before you leave Bangkok. I will send the car eight o'clock.' She hung up before anything more could be said.

The car arrived punctually. There were two men in it: an interpreter and a man who knew the way to the temple.

We arrived an hour later and threaded our way through the narrow alleyways that led to the temple, and up over a high, arched Chinese bridge. People stared curiously as we passed, and smiled and bowed over the top of their exquisitely arranged fruit and vegetables. The temple was whitewashed like all the others, but in a more dilapidated condition.

A monk showed us into a small room furnished with a lacquered Thai cabinet and some green plastic chairs.

After a little while which seemed long because of my anticipation, an old man entered, smiling and gracious, followed by four monks, one of whom was an Englishman and one a Negro. The orange of their robes was blinding as they sat down on the remaining chairs, facing us.

The abbot, as I called him since I didn't know the correct name for the head of a monastery, began to speak:

'I have been expecting you. How can I help you?'

'Can you explain to me the teaching of Buddhism?' I asked him.

'I will try. You will understand if you are ready. Many come asking the same question but they interpret what they hear according to their own way of thinking, their own prejudices, and go away disappointed. Try to forget all you have learned and listen to my words as if they are the first you have heard. Does your way of life satisfy you?'

'No.'

'Why not?'

'Because it is incomplete.'

'How incomplete?'

'Empty of meaning somehow, without purpose.'

'Do you believe it has no purpose?'

'No, I feel it has one but I don't know what it is. Can Buddhism give me the answer?'

'The answer is always available to those who seek with their whole heart, but the practice of Buddhism, unfortunately, like that of Hinduism and Christianity is degenerate. East and West men are preoccupied with what is trivial, passing, without value.'

'But how can one say what has value in this present world? That is the whole problem.'

'Only one thing has value: Enlightenment.'

27

'Does Enlightenment mean Nirvana?'

'Yes.'

'But doesn't that mean annihilation and the death of the soul?'

'Not of the soul, but of ignorance and separation.'

'But I have read that the Buddha did not believe in any permanent entity or essence like the Real Self: that Nirvana is an experience of bliss followed by utter dissolution; that He denied the existence of both God and the soul.'

'That is the interpretation given to Buddhism by men who have understood neither the teaching nor themselves.'

'Why did he say that everything was unreal?'

'Can you say of what passes through you, of your fleeting emotions and thoughts, of the circumstances that come to you, this is I; this is permanent; this is real?'

'No, I suppose not.'

'Do you know what is permanent and real?'

'No, unless God is, but I don't know that God exists. Did the Buddha believe in God?'

'He didn't speak of God, which is different. If a man realizes God and is among other men who do not, it is useless to speak about Him for they would not understand. It is better to indicate how they may come to know Him themselves. Man must discover God and his True Self or Ego by following the Path to Enlightenment.'

'But how can I know God and the True Self really exist?'

'I will tell you a story which may perhaps answer your question. It concerns an interview between the Buddha and the monk Vachagotta.

'The wandering monk Vachagotta spoke to the Exalted One, saying: "How does the matter stand, venerable Gotama, is there the Ego?"

'When he said this, the Exalted One was silent.

' "How then, venerable Gotama, is there not the Ego?"

'And still the Exalted One maintained silence. Then the wandering monk Vachagotta rose from his seat and went away.

'But the venerable Ananda, when the wandering monk Vachagotta had gone to a distance, soon said to the Exalted One:

' "Wherefore, Sire, has the Exalted One not given an answer to the questions put by the wandering monk Vachagotta?"

' "If I, Ananda, when the wandering monk Vachagotta asked me: 'Is there the Ego?' had answered: 'The Ego is,' then that, Ananda, would have confirmed the doctrine of the Samanas and Brahmanas who believe in permanence. If I, Ananda, when the wandering monk Vachagotta asked me: 'Is there not the Ego?' had answered: 'the Ego is not,' then that, Ananda, would have confirmed the doctrine of the

28

Samanas and Brahmanas who believe in annihilation. If I, Ananda, when the wandering monk Vachogotta asked me: 'Is there the Ego?' had answered: 'The Ego is,' would that have served my end, Ananda, by producing in him the knowledge: all existences are non-Ego?"

' "That it would not, Sire."

' "But if I, Ananda, when the wandering monk Vachagotta asked me: 'Is there not the Ego?' had answered: 'The Ego is not,' then that, Ananda, would only have caused the wandering monk Vachagotta to be thrown from one bewilderment into another: 'My Ego, did it not exist before? but now it exists no longer!' "

'Knowledge by itself serves no purpose unless there is also experience of the truth.'[1]

'But how can one experience truth? What is truth?'

'Truth is the experience of Who one is.'

'But how can I discover who I am? I don't understand.'

'You have experienced everything many times in different lives: love, hate, desire, suffering. Each time, when you have begun to perceive a little of the truth, you have said, "Next time I will change; next time try to be free of the wheel of rebirth." But in each life you forget what you learned in the previous one and you cling to the desires and suffering of the present. You still do not realize that it is attachment to what does not belong to the Self that generates desire and suffering and ties you to the wheel of rebirth. The desire for things of life; for wealth, pleasure, power, love, draws you back into life. Purify your desire: attach it to the search for the Real Self and you can be free. Enlightenment is possible and not as remote as imagined.'

'But how can I purify desire?'

'By following the Noble Eightfold Path.'

'What is the Noble Eightfold Path?'

'The eight stages of this Path are like the eight spokes of the wheel whose centre is Enlightenment and Liberation. To be perfectly, completely enlightened, there must be, first of all, perfect understanding of the Buddha's Four Noble Truths; of suffering, the cause of suffering, the overcoming of suffering and the way which leads to the overcoming of suffering.

'For example, you have told me that you suffer; that you seek a way to overcome suffering. I have told you that the way lies through Self-discovery. Later you will understand more completely what this means. When you have fully understood the cause of suffering in yourself, you will begin to understand the way which leads to its overcoming.

[1] In other words, Vachagotta knew of the Ego only as an intellectual idea, not as an experience.

'From the complete understanding of the Four Noble Truths can come the remaining seven steps:

> perfect aspirations
> perfect speech
> perfect action
> perfect livelihood
> perfect effort
> perfect mindfulness
> perfect concentration

'This is the path of detachment and realization.'

'But that surely means withdrawing from life.'

'On the contrary, the path is to be followed in the midst of life. Grow like a tree, in the soil of earth.'

'Will it take long? Can I reach the end in this life?'

'Does a tree grow to its full height in a single season? Can a soul reach its full growth and perfection in one life? No, it is obvious that it cannot. Many lives of struggle and search and suffering are experienced before the soul awakes to realization of what its destiny is; and many more before it can become one with the Supreme Being. But if for ages there has been right preparation and effort, then in a moment, Enlightenment may be experienced.'

'Then what happens?'

'Then Samsara which is life as you know it now becomes Nirvana or life as it really is.'

'And can the Eightfold Path really lead to this?'

'If it is followed faithfully, yes. To walk in the Way is to encourage the soul to grow. As it grows it gains insight. As it gains insight, it understands, as it understands, it loves and as it loves it becomes what essentially it Is. There is only one obedience which is to obey the law of love. Detach yourself from what is impermanent. Then you will find the Permanent. You have a Christian saying, I believe: "What is a man profited if he gain the whole world and lose his soul?"[1] There is no more fitting summary of the Lord Buddha's teaching than these words.'

'Can you tell me what I should do to follow the Way which leads to Enlightenment – I mean how to follow it in my everyday life?'

'Concentrate first on freeing yourself from the illusion that the "I" or outer self exists separately from the Real Self and upon removing the doubts that arise in the mind as to the existence and efficacy of the Path to Enlightenment. Do not cling to rituals which are of no value

[1] Gospel of St. Matthew 16:26.

until you can understand their symbolism. Work strenuously to recognize and overcome anger, hatred and lust. These are the Lower Fetters which stand in the way of one striving to enter the Path.

'Learn to purify your speech; do not waste the breath of life in idle gossip, in the expression of restless thought which is harmful to others and useless to yourself.

'Substitute for the craving for existence the longing for experience of Reality.

'Work to make peace among men instead of fomenting strife by slander. Learn to have power over yourself by recognizing yourself as you are. Seek out the cause that leads you to acts of hatred and anger, to the hunting and killing of others' bodies, thoughts, ideas. Cultivate equanimity.

'Try also not to yield to sexual passions which, pursued for their own sake can lead you only deeper into Samsara.[1] Here, too, there should be balance.[2] You will find that when you take the first deliberate step towards this path, everything will be more difficult, your passions more violent, but if you hold steadfastly to your aim, you will pass through them and each time they recur, you will meet them with greater understanding of how to detach yourself from their grasp. Ultimately, you will no longer experience the desires that have led you away from your Self. Try to understand the mystery of sexual life and the symbolism related to it. When you have understood, you will be unable to abuse it.

'Overcome the desire to acquire fame in the world – for you will lose yourself and forget your true aim. Do not use the fire of the mind in useless competition with those who are asleep on the battlefield of life. Do not waste time in futile arguments about the value of this or that theory. Theories are only valuable if they lead to the Self. There is only one work – to find the Self.

'Do not lie to yourself. It is most difficult to recognize one's faults and more so to admit them. Pride is the veiler of Truth. Do not allow pride to rule you. Seize the Dragon and overcome the great fear. You will struggle to choose between striving after wordly powers and cultivating your own innate spiritual powers. Watch and you will overcome.

'Lastly, seek out in yourself all aspects of coveting and ignorance for these two are the root-cause of all your wandering in the lower worlds. See how they enslave others and hold humanity in bondage to illusion.'

[1] Samsara is life bound to the Wheel of Karma, or the law of cause and effect, sowing and reaping. Nirvana is life lived in freedom from this law.
[2] Implying control, not abstinence.

31

'How should I overcome these?'

'When held by desire to the lower forms of life strive to remember your True Desire. Renounce what does not belong to you. Desire only what does. Then will desire become your servant instead of your master.'

'Do you mean I have to withdraw from life?'

'Again you ask me the same question. Again I say no. If you do not act in the midst of life, you cannot learn.

'You have need of the experiences gained in the world for this work. Rather pass through the midst of life longing not for wealth or fame or power or love but only for the experience of Reality. Do not be waylaid and diverted by your lesser desires. Put what is of paramount importance first. The last desire is for liberation and the last barrier the idea of personal attainment. When these have passed away you will have overcome Death and awoken to Life.

'You will soon discover what a joy it is to realize that the Path to Freedom which all the Buddhas have trodden is ever-existent, ever-unchanged and ever open to those who are ready to enter upon it.

'You will realize that the outer world that you weep and despair over is the reflection of the battlefield in your own soul. The greatest service you can render the world is to know yourself.

'Finally you will have penetrated the meaning of the words: "Not by any travelling is the world's end reached. Verily I declare to you that within this fathom-long body with its perceptions and its mind, lies the world, its arising and its ceasing and the way that leads to its cessation." '[1]

I tried to remember and sat in silence, feeling the horizon of possibility drawing near.

The abbot spoke again.

'Come,' he said, 'I will take you into the Lord Buddha's House.'

I followed him into the Hall of Meditation. It was a long rectangle with high windows letting in the light through two of the walls. A gilded statue of the Buddha towered at one end of it. In front of Him was a large dais that filled most of the room, raised about a foot above the ground. Monks began to come into the hall and to arrange themselves in rows on the dais, facing in the same direction as the abbot. At his feet sat a boy of twelve. I sat opposite them, on the floor by the dais.

Putting his hand on the boy's shoulder, the abbot said to me: 'He is close to Enlightenment though only twelve. I have asked him to take

[1] From the Samyutta Nikaya ii; 3, 6. Quoted by Sri Krishna Prem in *The Yoga of the Bhagavad Gita* (Watkins).

you with him, as we pray, into the inner worlds.' The boy smiled at me and I smiled back, as the abbot began to pay out from his hand a long white cord that eventually was held by every monk in the hall. Then, intoning some words from the Dhammapada, or Book of the Law, in the rhythm and tone of a chant, he drew me with him, repeating the words of the prayer, until the hall vibrated with the sound of fifty voices intoning in unison.

I forgot to look at the golden image of the Buddha or at the beautiful unemaciated bodies of the monks in their orange robes, or at the remarkable faces of the old man and the boy, or the cord that shone like a ribbon of light in fifty hands. I closed my eyes and listened and went deeper, deeper, deeper into the chanting. It dashed against my hearing in great waves, now with the roar of a breaker crumbling, now with the softness of water being withdrawn into the sea.

'This is prayer,' I thought. 'Not the mechanical repetition of formulas but the great Affirmation of Being.' The words came into my mind without my searching for them. A hand on my shoulder brought me back to the outer world.

'The abbot wishes you to wait for him in the little room.'

I found it a tremendous effort to get up off the floor and to leave the hall where the prayer was still being intoned.

He came to us in ten minutes.

'That was an extraordinary experience. Is it always like that?'

'By no means, but it could become like that always.'

'Is Nirvana like that?'

'Nirvana is far beyond, but this could lead you to it. You will stay?'

'Stay?' I echoed.

'Yes, you are ready to go further. It will help you to stay here for a few months.'

'But I can't stay. I have to return to my work in England.'

'What work is more important than this?'

I felt the panic of indecision rise in me, saw myself caught between duty and desire.

'I will come back.'

The abbot smiled at me and my companions. Then he rose and left. The room was empty.

We went out of the temple and felt the same sensation as when there is suddenly noise after long silence. But we were all happy.

'It was wonderful, wasn't it?' the interpreter exclaimed. 'I never understood properly before.'

Was it possible that Buddhists did not understand their own religion? I wondered.

We laughed with the sheer delight of having shared the experience. Gone was the polite indifference. We had all been vitally involved together.

We stopped on the way to the car to buy some rice that had been baked in a bamboo cylinder. The interpreter bought and handed it to me, showing me how to peel off the bamboo and find the warm, damp rice inside.

Part Three

I WONDER WHY I DID NOT STAY. WAS THIS A MOMENT of choice and did I let it slip by? The step was too big to make; the fetters holding me too strong. I was not sure that this was the Way. I did not really understand what the abbot said. Only the essence of his words remained and the experience in the Meditation Hall. The notes I made were incoherent. Without the strength of his presence, I wavered. Besides, India was ahead – unknown. There would be time later to learn how to meditate, how to purify desire. Now there was too much to experience. And had he not said: do not withdraw from life? Life in a monastery seemed to imply withdrawal. I did not know that periods of withdrawal – a day, a month, a year perhaps – are necessary if one is to learn how to breathe in the world, how to bring down the understanding gained on the mountain tops to the level of everyday life.

So I turned West, towards India.

I entered Calcutta alone and saw for the first time the prototype of Indian cities: the thick-crowding of streets with too many people; the inching of cars through a maelstrom of bodies, bare feet, striped pyjamas and white dhotis; street stalls piled high with food and merchandise; refuse cluttering the gutters; shopkeepers crying their wares and beggars barring the way of entry into their shops. In the midst of this, women glided calmly, seemingly unmoved by turmoil, unstained by filth. Only they and the mangy, bone-thin cows that held their places in the middle of the streets were imperturbable.

There were buildings of all kinds: the decaying mansions belonging to the days of the British Raj, now infected with dirt or altogether abandoned; modern business blocks; hotels with their quota of American tourists and business men; dilapidated sections of the city where the not-so-poor lived and had their shops; and areas infested with thousands of shacks, which clung to the outskirts of the city like flies to a sticky sweet, where emaciated bodies crouched to escape the heat of the sun.

At night the streets were lined with recumbent people whose faces were turned to the wall and whose legs and feet protruded spikily. I was ashamed to look at them because their condition seemed beyond all hope of help.

They didn't seem like human beings, but like a thousand lumps of mud scattered by the furrowing of a plough. I looked furtively at the dusty soles of feet worn too thin by hunger and disease, yet too large for the bodies they belonged to. I felt guilty, because I saw that all the emotions of sympathy, sorrow, pity were completely useless. What could I do about them? What could be done to help them? There were so many.

The weight of violence was great in Calcutta. Perhaps it was because there were so many people thronging the streets in search of work and food – mob-ripe. By day the buildings shivered with the din that rose from the streets. By night, I lay awake listening to the awful cries that echoed through the city. Who was attacking? Who fought for life? Who died?

★   ★   ★   ★

I went first to Rajputana, where the country is tawny and jungles of thick brush conceal the tigers and black panther that roam through them. I came upon its cities unexpectedly – as if a genii had waved them into being with his wand: Jaipur and Bundi; Ajmer and Jodhpur; Bikinir and Udaipur.

The shacks of the refugees that for ten years had made a shambles of the city streets were disappearing and I could peer into the interior of shops whose white plaster walls were hung with brightly coloured cottons. Jewellers still worked masterpieces with enamel and precious stones. Men wore the heavy rounded turban of Rajputana, dyed lime-green or scarlet or sky-blue. Women walked freely with many-pleated skirts swinging wide around their ankles above a pair of silver bangles. They did not have the terrible thinness of the people in Calcutta. It was impossible to imagine a people of greater dignity and beauty. They carried their past proudly.

Each city had an encircling wall and a castle-palace.

The palaces were immense – like the walled towns of Tuscany. Some had a melancholy atmosphere because they had been deserted by their Princes, but their magnificence was undiminished. There was rarely the grey stone of European castles against which the Alhambra is like a spurt of flame in the night. Instead, there was sandstone and marble, the salmon-pink confection of Jaipur, or pale ochre stone, as at Bundi or Amber, or the white of Udaipur. Inside were halls of ceremony, once spread lavishly with carpets and animated by a life of luxury and splendour and violence. There were rooms of repose,

36

painted with birds and leaves and foliage, or lined with fragments of mirror so that they scintillated with every refraction of light. There were gardens for the hours of the day; and balconies for the night, overlooking lakes or rivers; and the honeycombed prisons of the zenana.

Looking back over my life as I wandered through them, I saw an endless vista of castles. From the time when, as a child, I had shaped their crenellations in sand, they had been to me a symbol of power – not tyranny to be resented and destroyed but strength to be emulated. This had been in my mind when I discovered the sky through the alabaster windows of the Alhambra and felt the magic of fountains; and when, in the chateaux of Provence and Aquitaine, I had relived a life of sun and poetry, where women waited among flowers. Like them, I feared the cruelty of the men of the north who had only fires to warm their hearts, and of the men of the south to whom cruelty should have been alien but who made it an art – who, in defence of an empty tomb, carried their fierce passion to Syria and enthroned it in Krak, high above the desert and the rock. Why had they mistaken death for life?

Of all the castles of Rajputana, it was only to Udaipur that I longed to return. To it alone belonged the two lines of poetry engraved on the white marble hall in the Red Fort at Delhi that had once contained the Peacock Throne.

'Be there a Paradise on earth, oh it is here; it is here; it is here.'

At Udaipur the line between history and legend was very fine and mind and heart were close, spliced by wonder.

The palace of the Maharanas, who claim descent from the sun and precedence over all the other rulers of Rajputana, was on a hill at the far end of the city. It had the smell of the long abandoned, but high up was access to beauty. Alabaster balconies revealed a glimpse of gold cupolas below. From lattice windows walls plummeted hundreds of feet to the lake beneath, and the whole palace, like the city, was white. Around the shores of the lake was a frieze of trees and temples. Far out on the water were three island pavilions. Beyond them, on the further shore was a line of pink and amber hills and to one of them on its very summit, clung a castle.

I was rowed out to the most remote and beautiful of the pavilions. From there the blue hills of Mewar seemed to encircle the lake-city like the forest in the story of the Sleeping Beauty. For hours I sat, gazing at this image of perfection as I would have held a pearl in my

37

hand, loving every facet of its iridescence. By day, the city belonged to the heroic world of the sun, permanently reflected in water. At night it was amorphous, then radiant as the wraiths of mist breathed round it by the water dissolved beneath the rays of the moon, until, with the approach of dawn, they returned to herald the geranium glow of day.

★　★　★　★

I approached Ajanta treading softly, expectant of wonders. It was very still. There was only the sound of water trickling far below in a ravine and the cry of hawks circling overhead. Everything else had been parched into silence by the sun.

Following a narrow path that wound upwards, I turned the shoulder of a hill and saw, extending away from me in a long crescent, a grey, withered cliff. I could see its steep plunge to the valley floor and half way up, phantasmagoric like the thinly opened jaws of a giant, the pillared entrances to the Caves.

Ajanta! Ajanta! So many times had I pronounced its name with awe and imagined its paintings. The place of concealment where for centuries they had remained undiscovered gave no intimation of what lay inside.

I knew that the twenty-nine caves had been hewn out of the rock between the second century B.C. and the seventh A.D. and that the finest paintings were on the walls of only a few of them – the rest being devoted to sculpture.

The books I had read contained many photographs and gave the history of discovery. They told how the frescoes, preserved intact and unfaded for many centuries, had been broken in pieces from the walls, exposed to sooty lanterns and dousings with water, and how the copies had been mysteriously destroyed by fire.

But the books did not explain where the artists had come from – whether from nearby Gujerati or far-away Peshawar; nor why they had chosen this secluded valley for their immense labour; nor why they had left, as if upon disaster, carrying with them their unsurpassed mastery of the art of painting.

So little is known about India during the first seven centuries and particularly about that part of India. It could have been sparsely populated with immense distances between cities, or it could have been rather as Spain was under the Moorish influence, where cities like Cordoba drew from far-away places any scholar sufficiently intrepid to risk the journey.

Ajanta was not very far from the west coast and could therefore have

38

been in contact by sea with other parts of the world. Like other remote monasteries scattered throughout Asia, it was a haven of refuge, learning and peace along the pilgrim roads.

Knowing little more than this, I was unprepared for the experience of Ajanta. Nothing I had read nor photographs I had looked at had given me an intimation of what I would actually feel when standing inside the Caves.

If I hadn't already known that the paintings told the story of the life of the Buddha, I might have thought they represented a palace of earthly delight, for there was nothing specifically 'religious' about them – except perhaps the great statue of the Buddha at the back of the Caves, which at evening was reddened by the last shafts of the dying sun. The light of the guide's lamp passed over each section of the walls as the sun illumines a valley previously shrouded by cloud, revealing great processions, hunting scenes, feasts in palaces, golden women embraced by their lovers or bathed and jewelled by their handmaids; ceilings garlanded with leaves and flowers, precisely mosaiced in squares; elephants moving ponderously. Each figure detached itself from the wall and performed the ritual gestures of dancing, sitting, eating, love-making or flying through the sky, impelled by an energy neither too great nor too little. It was the spectacle of a never-ending dance of life and love and beauty.

But as, again and again, I plunged into the cool darkness of the Caves from the breathless heat outside, and then back to grow warm before exploring the next, it slowly dawned upon me that the artists of Ajanta were absorbed in a personally experienced revelation. They knew what they were doing. Then suddenly, I saw the paintings from a different aspect – one more closely related to myself, speaking to the part that was always questioning. A current of heat stronger than that caused by the temperature rushed through me as I looked at scene after scene from the life of the Buddha – scenes as varied as the aspects of the life of any man, my own included – but where, instead of discord and confusion, all is harmony, light, rhythm, beauty and love.

I followed Him from His miraculous birth from His Mother's side, as she stood holding on to a branch of the sacred Bodhi tree, then to His life as a young man in His Father's palace at Kapilavastu – to which part belonged the processions, the feasts, the exquisite woman who sat beside Him as His wife, with ropes of pearls hanging between her breasts; and to the moment of His first awakening when He was taken through the streets of the city by His charioteer and saw there, for the first time with awareness, old age, sickness and death; then to His decision to leave the palace, without saying goodbye to His wife

39

and child, and the secret departure on His devoted horse, Kanthaka, whose hoofs were muffled by the Gods so that they made no sound. He went then from one Brahman teacher to another, for a period of six years, trying to learn from them the method of understanding the Mystery of Life, practising asceticism in its most rigorous forms, until He abandoned this approach as useless to achieve His aim. He remembered an experience of mystical contemplation that He had had years before as a child and decided to return to that method. So He sat beneath the Bo tree, 'earnest, strenuous and resolute', undeterred by the repeated temptations of Mara, until He achieved the state called Enlightenment.

To one fresco in particular I returned as often as I could secure the guide and his lamp for myself. It showed the Buddha as He was before he attained Enlightenment – as the Bodhisattva, or one who has set his foot upon the Path. He stood with all forces gathered in readiness; on His head a great pointed diadem; in His right hand a white lotus; His mouth curved into a smile of such certitude, of a joy so magnetic that it compelled in me the affirmation:

'Yes!' I cried. 'Now and forever a million times, Yes!'

I thought of other men's pronouncements on Buddhism – that it was a doctrine of pessimism and nihilism. Now at last, it was clear that Buddhism was the exact opposite of this and that the men who had written thus had drawn intellectual conclusions from what they had read; that they had seen and felt and understood nothing.

All theories faded. What I saw with pristine clarity was that the men and women, animals, flowers and foliage of Ajanta were alive with a greater 'being' than I; that they were animated by energy moving at a swifter rate of vibration than any I had experienced, or even imagined to exist.

The artists had taken their models from the soil of India – the women beside whom, even today, other women seem stiff and graceless, and the men whose natural attitude seems so often to be that of 'kingly ease'. From India they took their respect for animals and their love of beauty in all the kingdoms of Nature: mineral, vegetable, animal and human. They succeeded in transposing onto their walls the idea that beauty is to be appreciated because Great Beings have taken immense pains over the world; that beauty is a method of bringing the soul of man into contact with Them because it can evoke in a person an emotional state wherein he can understand intuitively what is incomprehensible to him when he is using his reasoning mind alone.

They showed me, as the abbot in Bangkok had told me, that Nirvana is the highest attainment possible for man, that it is an experience and

40

Bodhisattva, Ajanta (Photograph by courtesy of Madanjeet Singh)

not an intellectual idea, and that eventually, like the marvellous creatures of Ajanta, I or any man could reach that level of being; could while still in earth-life dance among the stars and love in another dimension, could feel the rush of cosmic winds and know serenity.

★   ★   ★   ★

I saw Bombay through a haze made luminous by a watery sun – an immensely long waterfront, a line of docks arranged like dominoes, toy ships floating on the metallic surface of the bay and a row of buildings which muffled the roaring city behind them.

In a large hotel in India there is hope of excluding the night sounds. In a small one there is none. Hour after hour I lay awake, rigid as a Crusader on his tomb, hands folded, feet pointed upwards, listening, listening for the first sounds of the milk distribution that started beneath the window at five o'clock. I rose early to forestall the horde of tourists which flowed daily across the soft, thick water to the mound-like islands where Elephanta lay hidden – a cave in the heart of a mountain.

A jetty of smooth stones led from the boat to land. The tide was out and the water shallow and swampy. Desiccated trees, seizing a root-hold in the ooze, stood half-drowned, sadly reflected in water.

I arrived at seven – the unexpected.

Suspending for a moment the effort of seeing that my feet contacted stone and did not slip into the water, I saw to my right, not more than four yards away, a white object, flung like a piece of hosing across the branch of one of the trees.

I took in the details one by one: the body hanging limply with its feet just touching the water; the arms extended as if for diving with the head lolling between; the leather belt and the immaculate white trousers that belonged to the world of shops and offices and not to the naked brown ankles that protruded from them, nor the pathetic up-turned soles of the feet.

I did not at first see the red blot between the shoulders and the knife handle stuck through the shirt. When I did see it, the realization seemed to last an eternity.

'Oh God!' I whispered to myself. 'Even here, at the threshold of a shrine, there is violence.'

We had all seen him now, including the boatman and the guide. Reaching the shore, we demanded that he should be taken down from the tree, that the police should be fetched, that we should take him back with us to Bombay. From the response we gathered in the care-

Buddha in the attitude of subduing Mara: Srivijaya style
(National Museum, Bangkok)

fully innocent faces of those on shore, there might have been no body. Certainly there was nothing to be done.

With others, I entered the cool gloom of the cave. The towering figures of protecting deities cast the weight of a thousand years of contemplation upon us. I came to the central shrine – a colossal, three-aspected image of the Hindu God Siva, manifesting here as the Creator, Destroyer, Sustainer of the Universe; manifested as the opposites and what lies between them, the reconciler. His gaze penetrated far into hidden worlds and I felt it engendering unimaginable creations.

Who is Siva? How can He create, destroy and sustain at the same time? What Universe is the sphere of His activity? Is He God? Or is Brahma God? But to these questions there was no answer.

The body was still there when we came out of the cave and walked down the long flight of steps to the jetty. Silently the hostile group of men stood watching us as we moved from stone to stone, until at last we reached the boat.

Slowly we crossed over the water to the further shore.

*　　*　　*　　*

These experiences gave me a focus for my enquiries. I wanted to learn more about the religions that had inspired the sculptures and paintings I had seen. When I arrived in Delhi, therefore, I asked where I might find someone who could explain them. I was given the name of a man who in the summer lived in Rishikesh, high up in the mountains, but who in the winter lectured in Delhi on the Bhagavad Gita.

I decided to go to one of these lectures and arrived before an immense tent, which in the day time was a school. The flaps were rolled up to admit the air. Inside were about five hundred people, well dressed and obviously well educated. The men sat on the left, and the women on the right, on the ground. On the rostrum, cross-legged, sat a bearded man, with dark hair falling upon a flaming orange robe. Smiling often, he spoke to us in clear, fluent English interpreting, verse by verse, a chapter of the Bhagavad Gita.

After an hour's lecture, he announced that we would all meditate. Instructing us mentally to prostrate ourselves before Whoever was our God – whether Siva, or Buddha, or Christ or Allah, he told us to try and relax our muscles and to let go of our thoughts as much as we were able to. Then he told us to say 'Om' aloud twenty-one times, and twenty-one times silently.

Doing as instructed, we repeated the syllable twenty-one times in unison, then to ourselves, and sat afterwards in silence, with eyes closed.

It seemed only a moment before there was a shuffling of people rising to go. In fact, three-quarters of an hour had elapsed.

The next day, I went to a house where he was teaching a small group of people. Entering the room, I sat down on the floor behind the others, waiting for an opportunity to speak. He was explaining that at a certain level of understanding the teaching of all religions was the same. 'Never,' he said, 'accept anything finally until you know it to be true by personal experience. Do not accept unquestioningly ideas imposed from without, until you have proved their value in practice.

'Is there anyone who would like to ask me a question?'

Haltingly, I stammered out the first one that came to me.

'How can I stop the talking in my mind?'

He turned to the others: 'Here you have someone from the West,' he said, 'in all probability ignorant of the teaching of India, yet with her desire to know the truth, this girl has seized upon one of the key questions. It is this kind of question that I can answer – not those about the validity of this or that interpretation of the Gita, nor about which religion is the true one. Her question comes from the heart.

'Consider,' he said, turning to me, 'your thoughts as a river, cease-lessly flowing through your mind. You have the choice of flowing with them and becoming lost in some distant sea, or of lifting yourself out of them onto the bank of the river, and becoming a spectator of what passes before you.'

'Thank you,' I said. 'That helps a great deal. May I ask another?'

He nodded.

'Why do men kill?' I was still haunted by what I had seen at Elephanta.

'They kill because, ignorant of the great power in their hearts, they try to wrest power from what lies outside of them; they want to destroy what they cannot possess or understand. The urge to destroy arises from ignorance of the Divine Nature in oneself and all other beings.

I did not understand and thought it would be too complicated to ask him to explain further. Instead I asked again.

'Why am I afraid to leave my body as I once did when I was twelve?'

'The darkness frightens you because you do not yet know the light. Find the light that will dispel the darkness. Fear and ignorance will then disappear.'

Part Four

PERHAPS THE UNDERSTANDING THAT CAME AFTER I had left India would have come sooner if I had stayed in Bangkok or in Delhi, but because only part of me was engaged in this search, and the rest was barely participating and hardly tolerant, I could not do so. There was the desire to visit more places in India, to study more closely its art and architecture, and to meet other teachers. I could not stay with one person until I had experienced contact with many more. That is perhaps in keeping with the type of mind that ever needs new fuel for its curiosity – be the object business, religion, people, theories or facts. It skates over the surface without penetrating deeply or allowing itself time to concentrate. It cannot hear clearly but gathers a fragment here and a fragment there and realizes suddenly that if only it had listened closely and waited and wondered, it could have understood ages ago.

If I did not stay, it was because I was not ready. The moment was not yet. It may be that I needed to gather more threads before I could sit down to weave my tapestry under the guidance of the Master-Craftsmen.

So I continued the journey.

Hundreds of miles to the south, there was a different India, moving with the more ancient rhythm of a Dravidian past, whose women wore the crisp silk sarees of Mysore and Bangalore and at dusk wound wreaths of flowers through their hair. There was less violence than in Bombay and Calcutta, a more leisured tempo of life and among university students an attitude of scientific enquiry and pride in the technological progress of India.

I went with one of them to Mamallapuram and Conjeeveram – the seventh-century capital of the Pallava Kingdom, but being ignorant of Indian history and art and of the extraordinary influence of this Kingdom on South-East Asia, this fact meant nothing. Mamallapuram had shrines open to the sun and sculptures that swelled with life and vigour. There was a temple by the sea that looked eastwards towards distant lands. The temples of Conjeeveram were heavy and dark and somehow unholy. I gazed uncomprehendingly at the Pantheon of

44

Hindu Gods, ignorant of their rôles and their meaning, repeating after the guide their strange-sounding names: Durga and Kali; Siva and Parvati; Ganapati, Vishnu and Brahma. Hinduism seemed a primitive, almost barbaric religion.

Now I see it differently. India is saturated with the symbolism of death and rebirth. The sun burns and kills and the sun gives life and fertility. The earth is harsh and man is between earth and sky, the pilgrim struggling to reconcile the two. Earth is beautiful and sky is beautiful and between are the mountains. Who will risk his life on their snowy precipices? Who will follow the path of the great Rishis[1] – who for five thousand years and more have shown the way? The Aryans came with their hymns but the Dravidians already knew the truth and the lingam which exists all over India is the ancient symbol of that knowledge.

Today there are multitudes of temples and multitudes of priests and rituals but the spirit is gone and the letter is dead, as it is in the West. There are a few true teachers and many charlatans, a few dedicated to following the way and many who put on the outer garb of sainthood, but are not saints. There are many asrams[2] but it is hard to find one that is not under the guidance of a man who has power but no wisdom, knowledge but no love. Those who follow these in blind faith and devotion often lose their emotional balance and become addicts of sensation. There is no dignity, no peace, no truth in these places. Yet they have to be tested by experience. How otherwise is one to learn discrimination?

Before I arrived there, I had imagined that religion holds a far more important place in people's lives than it does in Europe. Soon it was clear that this is indeed the case but not as I expected.

So far has the present practice of Hinduism fallen from the teaching of the Seers that it seems in some ways as bankrupt of truth as the practice of Christianity. Great sections of the people follow the rituals of Hinduism without remotely understanding what they mean, because the priests no longer know how to interpret them. Many others, influenced by western 'culture' and 'scientific' outlook have turned their back upon what they justifiably regard as superstition. Others, including many misguided foreigners gather round the self-styled teachers of the numerous asrams. The larger these groups are and the more fanatically devoted to their leader, the less able are they to offer guidance. A few find their way to the more remote asrams and there are fortunate

[1] Sage or Enlightened man.
[2] Centres where people live and learn under the guidance of a Guru or spiritual teacher.

45

enough to sit at the feet of a true Guru, but they can only do this if they are ready to understand his teaching. If they are not, they will not find him, or if they find him they will have no ears to hear what he says.

Here therefore, are glaringly revealed all the pitfalls that the unwary person is likely to fall into in the course of his search for a teacher. They may be stages that have to be passed through on the way but it is dangerous to linger too long in the uncomprehending practice of ritual; to mistake charlatans for sages, or to cling to religious attitudes that will not allow growth beyond them.

Yet in India there is also a climate of revelation, where quests can be pursued without ridicule and where it is recognized that however low the general level of understanding has fallen, there have always been men to teach the way. In India, there are still certain places venerated for centuries owing to the presence of a continuous line of Rishis.

Arunachala is such a place. Its name means the Hill of Light. For hundreds of years, from all parts of the peninsula, men have come to live as hermits in its many caves and to learn from the Rishis who taught at its feet. The people of South India have always worshipped it as Mount Sumeru, the centre of the Universe.[1]

I went there because I had been told of a man called the Maharshi[2] who was said to have been the last of these Rishis, and who had lived there until his death a few years before. The fact that he was dead made no difference because the people I had met who had been there told me that his presence was there still and that it was a place so extraordinary, so full of his love and his being, that it was worth any number of journeys to be there even for a few days.

From friend to friend I had gone, following the thread; first in England, then in Calcutta, and now finally in Madras. There I went to meet a woman who for years had lived at the foot of Arunachala, outside the asram, and who asked me to stay with her there. So it was that once again the decision was taken for me.

Miles before I came anywhere near Arunachala, I could see its faint outline, rising above the immense, flat, ochre plain that rushed away from it on all sides, broken only by low hills or weird, twisted escarpments. I noticed immediately the feeling of ancientness – as if the place were as old as the earth itself and had never been touched by flood or volcanic eruption. If there are places on earth that are centres of magnetic attraction, this was one of them. As I went nearer, it seemed that the city of Tiruvannamalai at its base and all the people working around it were like specks of dust on the surface of a gigantic mirror

Symbol of the True Self, God.   [2] Sri Ramana.

46

reflecting the light of the sun – so tremendous was the force of the mountain.

It was February and the heat weighed like a stone. Having found the house of my friend and left my luggage there, I walked the few yards to the asram compound and was received by the postmaster, who seemed to be the person in charge of the place. His name was Raja and he darted hither and thither like a dragon-fly, a small slim figure with a bald head and glasses slipping off his nose. With solicitude he brought me food, although lunch had long since been finished, and sat watching me with eager eyes as clumsily I manoeuvred rice from leaf to mouth with three fingers of my right hand, mixing it with dahl and washing it down with butter milk.

Meanwhile, I took in the details of the asram. It consisted of a number of straw-thatched huts inside a wooden fence. There was an eating hall, huts for sleeping, a small library, a hall of meditation which contained a full length coloured photograph of the Maharshi draped with flowered wreaths, a stable for cows, and finally a small temple dedicated to his mother, with a pool to one side of it. A few Europeans had houses nearby where they had lived for years, but since the Maharshi had died, many fewer pilgrims came there and the place had a deserted feeling.

Later in the afternoon Raja took me up onto the mountain, which rose immediately behind the compound. Left to myself, I stayed there until dark, watching the sun withdraw itself inch by inch from the mysterious plain. It set directly in front of me, a huge ball of fire whose flames reddened the whole sky. Hiding behind the twisted boulders it made them cast vast shadows, violet, deep purple and black. Slowly the plain greyed and lost life and the lakes scattered over its surface became turquoise. Around me I could hear the swish-swish of people from the town cutting the long grass and carrying it in great bundles down the side of the mountain. They sang as they worked, tunes broken into fragments by their effort and the rustling grass. Then came darkness and they fell silent. Together we followed the white stone path that led downward to the sound of people preparing dinner over their cow-dung fires, and the smell that I had come to look for all over India, a smell that, pungent and acrid, yet not unpleasant, I would always associate with dusk.

The next morning, I was woken at five by the sound of a man's voice chanting prayers to Siva outside the window. Quickly I dressed and went onto the mountain. Now the stone was cold, although I could feel the gathering of heat. Never before had I felt to the depths of my being an emotion akin to adoration for the sun.

47

That day my hostess arrived and the house was filled with her laughter and her bustling energy. She took charge of me at once, sending me always to the mountain at dawn and dusk, talking to me for hours about Bhagavan, as she called the Maharshi, and initiating me twice a day into the varieties of Madrasi curries.

She was about sixty years old. All the life in her was concentrated in enormous brown eyes and in her beautiful hands that she used to emphasize points in her conversation. She had the Indian habit of nodding her head to one side as she talked. She wore cotton instead of silk sarees and insisted that I did the same, saying that I would be much cooler than in my close-fitting western clothes. Her favourite position was to sit, legs folded under her, on the sofa of the shady screened porch where we ate our meals. From there, during the day, she dealt with her correspondence and directed her maid, Maimona, and in the evening, hour after hour, told me stories about Bhagavan and the people who had come to him for help.

She had brought with her a girl of about my own age, called Hansa. She was as beautiful as any of the women of Ajanta and I, who had never seen such beauty in any human being, could not take my eyes off her. She spoke only when it was absolutely necessary. Rarely, she thrilled us with an exquisite smile. She seemed too fragile for the world, withdrawn into a distant heart of love, there to be sought out with difficulty.

One night, we were sitting as usual after dinner, entranced by the stories we were being told.

'Why do you always tell us to go onto the mountain?' I asked Ma,[1] as I had been told to call her. 'Why is it so extraordinary?'

'When I first came here and was told to go always onto it or around it, I was sceptical, too. Bhagavan said that it was alive, that it was Siva, the Great God of the Hindu Trinity. "How can it be Siva?" I asked. "How alive?" And I dismissed it as a poetic image.

'Then one night, I was sitting with a friend on my terrace, looking at the mountain. Suddenly, at its very centre, I saw an enormous heart, and in it a blazing star.

' "What are you looking at?" my friend asked. Without turning my head, I said, "Look where I am looking and tell me if you see anything."

' "Good Heavens!" she cried, and together we watched until dawn. The next day I told Bhagavan about it. "And why not?" was his only comment. So you see, my dear, the mountain means something very special to me. You will find out that it has a meaning for you, too, before you leave.'

[1] This word means 'Love'.

48

Then she began to tell the following story and I fell once more into a trance that came partly from the magnetism of her voice, partly from the story itself.

'A friend of mine sent her court musician to me to see if Bhagavan could do anything to help him. She was very worried about him as he would sit and weep all day long, where before his playing had been the delight of her court. He had a beautiful face and a long white beard, of a type you have probably seen in the Moghul paintings, and I was very touched by his distress. But I was busy with many people at the time and the first day could not do more than give him some food. The second night, as I was preparing to retire, he said to me, "I cannot go to sleep until I have told you my story." So, although I was very tired, I didn't have the heart to turn him away. This was the story he told me:

'From boyhood he had always adored the Goddess Parvati – Siva's consort – and had faithfully observed all the rites connected with her worship. When he played it was for her, and if he received some inspiration, it was to her that he gave thanks. Then one night he had a dream. He dreamed that an old man with a marvellous face stood by his bed and spoke to him. "Come," he said, and obediently he rose out of his body and left it lying on his bed, asleep. The man took him by the hand and together they rose through the night like arrows speeding to a destination. Past myriads of stars they went until they reached the planet Mercury. There he was taught many things. The next night, the man again appeared and this time took him to Jupiter, and the following night to the Sun. He called to his guide, "You are killing me with this heat. I cannot bear it." But he reassured him and he found himself free of pain in a world of light. Then one night later on, he was taken to the furthermost star of all. They were walking together when in the distance he saw what he thought was a mountain of diamonds. But as they came nearer, he saw that it was a palace, studded with a million rubies and sapphires, pale moonstones and emeralds. They entered and there before them sitting on a lotus throne, were Siva and Parvati. He fell to his knees and begged her, "Please, never send me away from Your Presence." And she answered him, saying, "Since you love me so much, you shall return here every night as long as you tell no-one what you have seen." He promised that he would never speak a word of his secret and returned to earth and his body.

'For two years he returned every night to that distant star and was with his Goddess. He began to lose interest in life. His wife and children grew remote and his days were only a longing for the night.

' "But why are you so distressed?" I asked him.

49

' "I will tell you, I will tell you." He cried, rocking to and fro in his grief. "All was wonderful until one day my neighbour, who was jealous of me, provoked me into breaking my vow. 'Our holy man is always praying to Parvati,' he taunted me. 'One might almost think he saw her in his dreams at night.' One day I burst out, 'It's true, it's true I do see her and every night I go to where she sits enthroned with her Lord.' My neighbour was silenced but that night I lay waiting, waiting, my fear growing. No man came to me, and I lay alone, praying and weeping. So it has been until now. Please can you ask Bhagavan if he will help me. I would rather die than live as I am now."

'I calmed him down and the next day took him to Bhagavan and told him the tale. Later Bhagavan said to me, "All illusion, illusion; nothing is real but the Self. Let him find that."

'What could I tell the poor man? In the end I told him that Bhagavan said that he should look for the Self and that then he would be reunited with his Goddess.'

I took advantage of the pause that followed this story to ask the question that had been in my mind for some days.

'Several times, Ma, you have mentioned this teaching of Bhagavan's about the Self, and I have read about it in the pamphlets and books in the asram, but I don't really understand it. Can you explain it to me?'

'No, my dear. I would rather someone else did. Tomorrow evening, I will ask him to come and talk to you. He will be able to answer all your questions.'

All the next day, as I sat on the mountain or in the shade of the porch, I tried to collect my thoughts and to marshal my questions. I reduced them finally to one sentence that seemed to contain all the others.

In the evening after we had eaten, I went up onto the mountain and sat down on my favourite rock, facing the sunset. At last, noiselessly, as one who is used to touching the earth with reverence, he came along the path, bowed a greeting in the Indian way with hands touching each other in the attitude of prayer, and sat down on the rock facing me. Silhouetted against the glow of the western sky, I could see only his form and not his features, so that when he began to speak, I wondered whether his voice came really from him or from the mountain itself.

'I know that your desire is to learn more of Bhagavan's teaching,' he said. 'It may be that I can help you.'

'I long to know the truth about life; what is man and what is God and what is the purpose that unites them?'

'Then hold fast to your longing and I will teach you. You have been a wanderer in many lands and many traditions, looking always for the explanation that would make life comprehensible and full of purpose; looking for the One Truth, the One Hope, the One Beloved that could reconcile the opposites and make of life a song instead of a cry of despair.'

'I have searched but have found no answer.'

'What says Christianity?'

'That man is sinful; that his fate depends upon God's Will and God's Grace; that if he does good in life, he will go to heaven after death, or else to hell if he does evil; that Jesus came to save the world. But all this is without meaning for me.'

'Have you searched in the teaching of the Buddha?'

'A little.'

'And where does It lead, the Noble Eightfold Path?'

'To Nirvana.'

'And what is Nirvana?'

'I don't know.'

'Have you penetrated into the mystery of the Tao?'

'No.'

'Or consulted the Vedas and Upanishads?'

'Yes, but always without comprehension. Even the Bhagavad Gita, which I love to read, is obscure. All philosophies, eastern and western, are remote – formulas to be read but not lived, because I have not the key to their understanding nor to their application in life.'

'Perhaps you have not been ready to understand.'

'Yet I have longed and longed to know. Years I have spent in search. Are they all wasted?'

'No effort is wasted. It is the thousands of separate moments of search and effort that have brought you from indifference and complacency to confusion, from confusion to the overriding desire to know the truth. All the experiences of life have their purpose and are stages which must be passed through on the way to the light, but when the experience is complete, you are at fault to linger and fail to pass on to further tests and greater endeavours. Your life has not been wasted. There are many phases of truth to be experienced and assimilated before you reach the One which explains all the others. In relation to what has still to be learned, you are always a child.

'And now you wish me to tell you about Bhagavan's teaching. What have you learned of it so far?'

'That it concerns the Self.'

'What is the Self?'

'I don't know.'

'To everyone who came here asking for help, Bhagavan said, "Ask yourself who you are." Many went away angry or baffled and dis-appointed, but a few have understood.'

'But surely that is what I have been asking myself for years, and have found no answer.'

'Yet you have not given up. Who, then, are you?'

'I am I.'

'And who is I?'

'The person I am, sitting here, listening to you.'

'But who is that person?'

'I don't know.'

'Yet you feel.'

'Yes, I feel. I feel that I am ignorant, limited, separate and lost, and that there is a way not to feel all these things. That way I seek with my whole heart.'

'Has it ever occurred to you that you might have two natures, a human and a Divine, a dwarf self and a God Self? Have you not con-sidered that what you call "myself" is the lesser of these, and that you have totally ignored the Presence in you of the Greater?'

'Isn't that the teaching of the Buddha?'

'Yes, it is, and of Hinduism and Christianity also.'

'I have never really thought of myself in that way.'

'Then how could you realize that the whole destiny of man is to learn how to bring these two parts of himself into union, and that the experiences of life teach him infinitely slowly and painfully, to make himself whole. Was it not Jesus who said, "Blessed is the man who knoweth this Word and hath brought down the Heaven and borne up the earth and raised it Heavenwards"?'[1]

'I never realized that this was the meaning of Earth and Heaven.'

'Then how could you have had any sense of direction in your search?'

'I don't know except that I knew that somewhere the truth must exist. But is then this God-Self the soul?'

'No, you may think of It rather as Spirit – the Divine Essence that is called God.'

'Then what is the soul?'

'It is the intermediary between God and man, Inner and Outer, Heaven and Earth. It is asleep – a slave of the lower self until it begins to awake and to seek the Higher. The power of desire can turn the energies of the soul upwards or downwards. Understand therefore, that there are three in you; the Hidden Ruler, the messenger, and the

[1] From the Gnostic 'Book of the Great Logos according to the Mystery', quoted by G. R. S. Mead, *Fragments of a Faith Forgotten* (Watkins).

usurper of the Kingdom. The minions of the usurper are legion. The soul serves the usurper until the trumpet sounds to call his armies to do obeisance to the King.

'Again, know that there are three bridges between Earth and Heaven. The first is belief. That you have already. The second is self-knowledge. That you will acquire slowly. The third is understanding which will grow if your search remains as single-minded as it is tonight. The builder of all three, however, is love. Love is the force which moves all things. If it takes the form of desire for the things of the world, then he who loves in this way remains a wanderer in darkness. If a man desires to find the Light, then he becomes the Knower and in time will reach at-one-ment with God.'

'Then it is not enough simply to believe in the Presence of the Divine Self within us just as we have been taught to believe in the existence of God?'

'Is belief knowledge? Has belief been enough for you?'

'No.'

'Can you with honesty say that you know something before you have actually "seen" it, before it is as much a part of your experience as is the daily rising and setting of the sun? I will put it another way. What has this journey been to you – I mean the journey of your life?'

'Search.'

'And what is search?'

I thought hard for a moment, then replied, 'Work.'

'And work?'

'A form of devotion to an aim – love, I suppose.'

'And love, in our eastern terminology is the Rainbow Bridge. So you see, there must be work undertaken with love. Belief is not enough.'

'What kind of work?'

'Purification.'

'Purification?'

'The elimination by a constant but gradual process of all that does not belong to the Self.'

I was silent, trying to remember my life as I was living it. After a while I realized that it consisted entirely of movement from one extreme to another; from life to death and day to night; from desire to repulsion and elation to depression; from love to hate and certainty to doubt. All my life as I knew it was governed by the opposites, by what in the East is called the Law of Karma, where action and reaction, cause and effect follow one another inexorably, without control or direction by the will. 'As I am now,' I thought, 'I am a robot, a plaything of my impulses, past and present.' Aloud I said:

'But how can I know what to eliminate?'

'Learn to recognize your personality and to know that it does not belong to what, essentially, you are. Personality is the product of the actions of past lives, of heredity, environment, education, experience. It is an agglomeration of mental and emotional reflexes that you have acquired and developed. It creeps subtly into growth. You identify your consciousness with it and call it "I". It is hard indeed to detach yourself from it and to remember that your allegiance is to a Greater Self.

'Be careful, however, not to confuse personality with individuality. Personality is division, separateness and illusion – Maya, as my Brothers of the East call it – but individuality is the purpose of evolution. Be unique by being all the others and yourself as well. This you will achieve when you have united soul with Spirit. You will know then why it is the characteristic of all the Buddhas that they consider all sentient beings as their own self because they know that all sentient beings as well as their own self come from one and the same Suchness.

'At the present moment, instead of flowing freely from the Self from Whom all arises, your consciousness is muddied and diverted into feeble streams because it has to run through the delta of the personality. You must find the way back to the Source. Like the salmon you must mount the stream against the current.

'Remember always that there is nothing you cannot do if you so desire. There is nothing you cannot be if you so desire. There is nothing in the Infinite that you cannot aspire to, for desire is prayer, and as you pray for Enlightenment with your longing and your effort and your will, so you will slowly see and understand more about all things in the universe.

'To find the Self, to be united with the Beloved, is to become Who you are. That is the answer to Bhagavan's question.'

'But how should I go about this work in my everyday life?'

'By learning to use your will, your insight, your reason. Make of reason a servant instead of a God. All men have reason but few know how to use it. Few are Self-conscious. Concentrate upon the single aim of reaching the Self. "Aim at the highest," Bhagavan said, "and thereby all lower aims are achieved." This does not mean that you must withdraw from life, although it is good to retire from time to time. It means to remember in the midst of life what your aim is and therefore what is of greater importance. This is the way to detachment.

'It will help you to think of yourself at present as a multitude rather than one person. See how external events call forth now one person, now another; how your thoughts come without being summoned and

54

go without being dismissed, how they scatter like sand before wind. See how your energy goes forth in anger, fear, greed, self-pity, envy jealousy, self-justification, criticism, gossip and doubt; how you are the victim of a constant succession of petty tyrants who rule for a moment, a day, or perhaps months at a time. While they rule, you sleep.

'If you can see one of these taking control and can, in that moment, remember your true aim, and can repeat this process again and again, ultimately you will take away its power. Slowly it will be de-energized. And with every effort you make to remember the Self, It will be more able to penetrate your consciousness. The soul will awake more and more. The way will be clearer. You will cease to react automatically, to repeat patterns of behaviour over and over again, to be swept away by tidal waves of emotion. At first, of course, you will only be able to do this for a minute at a time, but even that minute will astonish you and strengthen your will to continue. Never struggle against the thoughts and emotions you wish to be free of. Rather remember your purpose and concentrate upon the desire to know the Self and act accordingly. Then will they fall away from you.

'Accustom yourself to look in every flower, in every face, in every star for the symbolism of these ideas.'

'But aren't there some elements in me that help rather than hinder? For instance, there is the desire to know, the desire to help, the longing to love.'

'Indeed, some parts of your mind and emotions are awake already; others are completely asleep; others wander in a dream state. Eventually, all can become avenues of approach to the Cave of Being, because all can teach you something. That part of you which attempts to observe and remember is called in our Hindu terminology the Dragon-Slayer. In the Gnostic writings, it is known as the one who takes the Pearl from the sleeping Dragon. In your tradition, it is Michael, Captain of the Hosts of the Lord, and it is Jesus, the Saviour of Being. In the Egyptian teaching, it is Isis who goes searching throughout Egypt for the parts of the dismembered body of Osiris. When all parts have been reassembled, reorientated, Osiris is resurrected, reborn.

'This reassembling of yourself is a series of sacraments, to be performed with love. It is with love that this immense labour is undertaken; with love and gentleness it should be pursued. There must be no violence. It is a work that requires patience, the will-power to accept and surrender; fortitude, courage. With love you will learn to sacrifice to the Self what formerly you have clung to in ignorance, until you are emptied of all lesser desires.

'In India, the most trivial actions of everyday life were given a sacramental value. They used to serve as reminders to a person, teaching him that it is useless to expect the Self to do all the work; that his conscious participation in these activities is required. It is not enough to repeat formulas of dedication in the morning and then to go through the day in forgetfulness, doing what has to be done with hands or brain or mouth mechanically, without love. Eventually, after long practice, it happens that every thought, word and deed is consciously dedicated to the God-Self, so that it becomes impossible to think speak or do anything that is unworthy of Him.

'There is this verse that may help you to understand that all that you are is from this One: "I am thou and thou art I and wheresoever thou art, I am there; in all I am scattered, and whencesoever thou willest, thou gatherest Me; and gathering Me, thou gatherest Thyself."[1]

'Hitherto you have regarded yourself as whole and complete, with God the Creator outside yourself. You have been ignorant of the fact that God cannot be known except through the progressive union of man with the Divine Essence within him. You have been a person without responsibility, direction, or the power of choice, except that you have had the choice between darkness and light. Or perhaps at times, you thought that you had "rid yourself of superstition" as so many proudly proclaim today, and imagined that you were master of your destiny. Truly you have been master of nothing.

'Henceforth, you will see yourself not as one, but as two; Higher divided from lower, one part seeking the Other, the many seeking the One. When you have attained to the Second Birth of Self-realization, then will the many again become One. The way to Nirvana, the ancient, ancient Path, is Tao. When illumination is experienced, then is it seen that Samsara and Nirvana are One, that Heaven and Earth are One, that Spirit, soul and body are One, and everything is God.'

'Slowly I begin to understand this teaching. Tell me, please, when I have begun to follow this Path in earnest, does it require many more lives before the Self is experienced?'

'That I cannot answer, child. It depends upon the intensity of your aspiration and the difficulties to overcome. The concept of many lives is for some a release from hopelessness. It gives possibility. Anyone who has begun to understand this teaching perceives that the road is long and that one life is too short a time for the soul to reach union with the Spirit. The deeper the sleep of the soul, the more laws it is bound by, the more rigid is the operation of the Law of cause and effect. But with each effort to awake, to learn, to become Man, a fragment of a new

[1] From the Gnostic Gospel of Eve quoted by G. R. S. Mead in *Fragments of a Faith Forgotten* (Watkins).

Sesshu (1420-1506): Winter Landscape
(From *2000 Years of Japanese Art*, by courtesy of Thames and Hudson)

Angkor: The Bayon (author)

pattern is created which, by the same Law, brings the soul nearer to the Kingdom of Heaven. If there is no reflection born of experience and suffering, no longing, no effort, the soul will remain a slave, life after life, endlessly repeating the same patterns of existence, ever reaping what it has sown in the past. If no new seed is sown, there can never be a different harvest. Heaven and Hell are not states or places entered after physical death. Heaven can be experienced in life. No amount of physical dying will give you the right to enter it. Hell is the eclipse of the Spirit by a personality, which, through ignorance or fear, denies Its Presence.

'Go back to your books and compare the traditions of different races. See how everywhere the same teaching is clearly laid down for one who has eyes to see and ears to hear. See also how this teaching has been distorted, falsified, twisted to serve the purposes of the lower self. You have, all around you in the world, people who, through ignorance, ambition, fear, jealousy or complacency, cannot recognize the Presence of the Self. They are asleep. Some desire to awake but do not know how. Others know intuitively from the time they are born.

'This is an Age of Choice. Unity at every level has to become the Law of the earth. Those who respect it and make it their own will enter the Kingdom of Heaven. There is no longer any place for half men or sleeping men. Either you are a Complete Man or no man at all. When the time of Choice has passed, wretched will be those who did not awake in time to realize that all who seek knowledge must consciously serve the Lords of Compassion.

'You have many sciences but you have overlooked the only real Science. The others should serve It. Unorientated, they are dangerous. Orientated, they would have a hundred times their present effect. Look at the world and ask why knowledge is being sought, for whose sake there is search and struggle. What true use is made today of the immense creativeness and energy of man? What ends do they serve? With what national pride does he carry his ingenuity into outer space when on earth he has not yet fed the hungry, nor comforted those who weep.

' "Is there a God?" the people ask. "Has He forsaken us? Where should we look for Him? In the churches? In books? In nature? In the state? In scientific progress? In a rose? Should we search at all? Is not the need for God perhaps a monstrous deception, born of man's love of power? Who will tell us the truth?" Who indeed! Not the churches, nor the politicians, nor the industrialists or scientists; nor even the artists and poets. Who then will comfort the soul and replace slogans by ideas? Who will teach men how to help the world? Who will cease struggling to control matter and work instead to control himself? Beware, child, of answering these questions until you have answered your own; yet search out the answers to your own because you desire to put an end to the suffering of others.'

'But how can I really help?'

'Bhagavan said that the highest form of service you can render the world is your own Self-realization.'

'But that seems so selfish. Is there nothing I can do in the meantime?'

'Of what use are you to the world as you are now, being as you have described yourself, ignorant, separate, desolate and lost? And how much more use you could be when you know how to help, when the whole force of your united being is flowing in one direction – outward – in love for man.'

'But it must take such a long time; I need such patience, such determination. Am I strong enough?'

'All who pass this way ask the same thing. Be assured that the Eternal Quest must come to Its goal and the discipline of creation must be learned by every individual. Remember that you desire to help the world. That will give you courage and perseverance. Your lives so far have been a childhood. They have seen the gathering of multitudinous threads for the weaving of tomorrow's beginning. If you falter, remember that tomorrow's Robe of Glory is woven of the threads you spin today. By infinitesimal efforts, day by day, hour by hour, you will reach the end of the Path.'

'Can you tell me one last thing, why did Bhagavan attach so much importance to the mountain?'

'Because it is the symbol of all that I have tried to explain to you tonight. The ascent of the Holy Mountain is the search for the Higher Self, the Great Purusha in the heart. All revelations take place on the Mountain. The Holy Mountain is within you. In you lies the Way, the Truth and the Life. Have not the great teachers of mankind, speaking from all the corners of the earth, taught this again and again? That is why Bhagavan told people to ask the Mountain their questions, knowing that It would teach them all they needed to know. "To see God is to be God," he said.

'I will give you one verse from the Upanishads to remember, lest you forget the rest. This you will not forget because you are already familiar with the symbol:

'The One Swan is in the heart of the world;
He verily is the Fire that has entered into the waters.

Having known Him one crosses over Death;
There is no other Path for going there.'[1]

With this he rose, and smiled at me, and walked into the night.

★   ★   ★   ★

The path around the Mountain, which all who go to Bhagavan have to tread, is nine miles long. We set out at five o'clock when the sun is still very bright. Hansa goes with me. We walk for a long time without speaking, trying to shield our faces from the powerful rays with the folds of our cotton sarees. Speech is unnecessary, so intense is the communion between us. Hansa, as she walks, becomes all Beauty, and as she raises her hand to shield her eyes from the sun, the tinkle of her gold bracelets is the only sound on earth.

I begin to think about the evening before, but as I look to the Mountain on my right, thoughts fall away. I begin to feel my smallness, and at the same time, strangely, my greatness. All solutions are inadequate. I cannot as I am eliminate suffering and despair from the world, nor even solve my own problems. I am not free to think or act in the way that an arrow speeds to its target. My only concern should be to learn how to apply what I have been taught, what has at last been opened to my understanding. Has not Bhagavan said that the greatest form of service one can render the world is one's own Self-realization? 'Aim at the highest and thereby all lower aims are achieved.'

With this thought comes a flow of energy that makes my feet speed over the ground like Hermes', hardly seeming to touch it. The golden plain stretches away to the left towards a line of violet hills. We speed past the five different faces of the mountain and our path is lit by the sun and the moon. We feel no fatigue. For each of us, no landscape has ever held such beauty nor any day such joy. Four hours after we have started, exultant, laughing, we run into Ma's garden, up the steps of her house, and into the inner room where she smilingly awaits us.

There is no further going.

[1] From the Shwetashwatara Upanishad VI:15.

Part Five

I

AFTER THE JOURNEY THERE IS THE RETURN, AFTER THE climb the descent, after the moment of insight the years of assimilation.

Who, during these years does not doubt? And because he is unsure of his revelation, feeling it to be remote, not yet part of himself, who will not go in search of more experience with which to test its validity?

I went again to India and the Far East, eager to touch the flame of beauty that seemed to burn more brightly there.

And then returned once again, this time with the desire to understand more fully what I had seen and loved.

'Go back to your books,' I had been told. 'Compare the traditions of different races. See how everywhere the teaching is the same.'

'Is it necessary to understand the texts?' I ask.

And You answer: 'You have been given the key. Use it. Grow; Learn; Love.'

This was the work of these years – to transform what had been stones into bread. Doing this work, seeing words with new eyes, beginning to understand what had once been incomprehensible, I wonder how I could have lived so long on stones and not starved to death.

God is still unknown but no longer unknowable.

I turn to Hinduism and Buddhism and find the word Enlightenment no longer baffles. I know it means seeing truly into the nature of God, which is at the same time, my own nature. Whether I call this experience Nirvana, Samadhi, Satori or the Kingdom of Heaven makes no difference. All describe the experience of insight into and becoming one with God, Who in various traditions is called:

Reality	Consciousness
That	Being
Atman	Non-Being
The Void	Infinity
The Full	OM
The Self	The One
Brahman	The Father
Bodhi	Truth
The Undifferentiated	Tao

60

I know this experience comes at first in separate moments of illumination and that only at the end is the seeker one with the Sought.

It is clear now that Enlightenment does not imply the annihilation of being, consciousness and existence and that it is not to be reached by renouncing life. I wonder how I could have thought that Nirvana and Samadhi meant a trance-like sleep or death.

I read fragments like this: 'Steady in the state of Fullness which shines when all desires are given up, and peaceful in the state of freedom in life, act playfully in the world, O Raghava! Inwardly free from all desires, dispassionate and detached, but outwardly active in all directions, act playfully in the world, O Raghava! Outwardly full of zeal in action but free from any zeal at heart, active in appearance but inwardly peaceful, work playfully in the world, O Raghava! Free from Ahankara; with mind detached as in sleep, pure like the Ether, ever untainted, act playfully in the world, O Raghava! Conducting yourself nobly and with kindly tenderness, outwardly conforming to conventions but inwardly renouncing all, act playfully in the world, O Raghava! Quite unattached at heart, but for all appearance acting as if with attachment, inwardly cool but outwardly full of fervour, act playfully in the world, O Raghava!'[1]

Does this imply trance-sleep, death or a renunciation of the world?

Rather I see that I must learn how to experience God in the very midst of life. An Enlightened man is one who has not renounced the world, but only the limited way of seeing it. He has managed to transfigure it. He sees it differently because he has 'overcome' or gone beyond the normal way of seeing it. Clearly he has broken through into a more complete and developed state of consciousness than the one I now know.

Sometimes, rarely, I stand on the brink of this experience. Long before God is known, He is felt. I realize that Enlightenment is an immense expansion of consciousness rather than an annihilation of it. The drop of water will one day contain the ocean, or perhaps be lost in it, according to which image is preferred.

God, the True Self, cannot be defined, only experienced. That is why He is called 'inconceivable and inscrutable; neither existent nor non-existent; neither phenomena nor noumena'.

My consciousness as it is now can never know God because He is beyond time and space and therefore beyond the part of the mind that thinks in time-space terms. He is everywhere at every second, but I

[1] From the Yoga-Vasishta, quoted by G. H. Mees, *The Revelation in the Wilderness* (N. Kluwer-Deventer); this passage was specially selected and translated by Sri Ramana Maharshi.

cannot yet experience Him everywhere at every second. I can say 'God is omnipresent', can think it, believe it, but I cannot become God consciously even for a moment.

How can I get outside time and space and learn to live in a part of the mind that works at a faster rate of vibration, more swiftly than time? How can I live in Eternity while still a part of the world of sensory perception? How be one with God so that my speech, thought, action reflect Him?

There is a part of the mind, usually called the intuition, which can reflect God and experience Eternity. It is this that works 'like lightning', 'in the twinkling of an eye', 'quick as a flash'. It is this part that is at work when an idea 'suddenly comes' and what was incomprehensible before makes sense.

In order to learn to live in this other part of the mind, or new level of consciousness, I have to learn how to detach myself from the empirical mind's way of thinking, and since action is the reflection of thought, of living.

Eventually I will be able to break through time into Eternity, and at a later stage will be able to live constantly in Eternity, while still a part of 'this world'. I will be one with God and because I am one with God, my speech and action will reflect God.

I am like a many-storied house. I live in the basement or the ground floor until I realize there are stairs leading to the roof.

The empirical consciousness is the ground floor. The intuitive consciousness is the middle. God-consciousness is the roof.

To climb the stairs is to move from one level of consciousness to another; to change from being man into being God.

All the sacred literature of India, from the Vedas, through the Upanishads, to the treatises on Yoga and the Buddhist sutras, teaches the method of inner growth which leads to the experience of Enlightenment.

The whole purpose of Yoga which is the Science of Union, is to teach man how to expand his consciousness from the circumference to the Centre; so that self becomes Self and man is united with God.

Hinduism and Buddhism teach that there are two paths for me to follow; one is that of the Fall into 'matter' which implies the progressive loss of insight into the nature of God or Reality with all the loss of control over thought, emotions and action which this involves. The True Self or God is by this Fall sheathed in progressively dense 'layers'. It is 'hidden', 'buried', lost'. As long as I imagine that my empirical consciousness represents my true self, the Real Self must remain unknown to me.

The other path is that of the Return to the Source through these veiling layers. As I climb this ladder, I progressively 'die to myself' – that is, I have to give up all the prejudices, passions, habits, limited ideas and ways of acting that belong to my lower, unpurified, unenlightened self. This self is called in Hinduism 'ahankara'. As I die to myself, I am reborn in God. I become increasingly aware of my True Nature. Finally, the two become One. There is no longer lower and Higher, outer and Inner. The illusory, separate self is annihilated. It is, I now see, to this death that the texts refer and not to physical death or to extinction of consciousness. When the death of the lower self has taken place, I am Awake, Enlightened, Anointed. I am Krishna; I am Buddha; I am Christ.

The science of Yoga teaches that the path of Return to the Source leads upwards through seven (sometimes condensed into five) levels of consciousness. These in Hindu and Buddhist terminology are called chakras (centres of force) or padmas (lotuses). It is taught that they correspond to the elements. To make their relationship clear to me, I arrange them as follows:

the muladhara chakra or padma (sensory perception physical body)	earth
the svadisthana chakra or padma (emotions)	water
the manipura chakra or padma (lower mind)	fire
the anahata chakra or padma (intuition)	air
the visuddha chakra or padma (insight)	ether
the ajna chakra or padma ⎫ (God consciousness)	moon
the sahasrara padma ⎭	sun
(the thousand-petalled lotus)	

There are, it is taught, various ways of raising consciousness through the seven levels and of achieving this Union, yet none is really complete in itself.

There is Hatha-Yoga, consisting of postures and exercises for the body; Bhakti-Yoga which teaches the purification of the emotions through devotion to and love of God; Raja-Yoga which is focused upon mind-purification and Jnana-Yoga which is the way based upon intuitive realization of the truth. There is Karma-Yoga, called the way of action, and Dhyana-Yoga, the way of meditation.

Yet all of these conceal a deeper meaning which is only apparent after much wondering and search for it.

All must be followed, at one time or another, in order to experience Enlightenment. Concentration in one direction inevitably has an effect on all the others. There can be no meditation unless there is knowledge of what to meditate about; no intuitive perception of truth without mind-purification; no mind-purification without the desire to love and serve God; no progress unless the body co-operates and is healthy and strong and no means of growing at all unless there is action at all levels. I cannot achieve Union by contemplation alone or action alone. There must be development on all levels and the harmonious co-operation of all faculties. None of this is a forced growth. As long as there is one-pointed desire towards the experience of God or Reality, there will be natural growth. No-one need say dramatically: 'I will renounce the world.' He will simply find that higher desires are slowly replacing lower ones and that he takes pleasure in a different kind of activity.

It is so easy to interpret literally the texts that discuss these different forms of Yoga. Yet it is soon obvious that the Hatha-Yoga texts in particular need a key and that their instructions have a symbolical as well as a literal meaning. The body, for example, is not necessarily the physical body alone, but the entire seven-storied being that I am. To interpret them on the level of the physical body alone may lead me far away from the path to be followed. It becomes clear that no amount of working on the physical body, of exercising, posturizing, cleansing the intestines or the digestive tract can by itself bring about Enlightenment. The ability to wash the intestines or lengthen the tongue is not a sign of spiritual development.

Again, what does Dhyana-Yoga mean? Does meditation mean only sitting in a quiet place, calming the mind and contemplating the Infinite, or does it mean the practise of recollection of aim in the midst of whatever my activity in the world may be? Is meditation something apart from life or is it the cultivation of a moment by moment awareness of God which can transform life into love?

Similarly with Pranayama or breath-control – does it really only apply to control of the physical breath or is there a deeper meaning? The answer is in the Tejobindupanishad: 'Man's Karmas come to an end when he realizes that everything he has a conception of is but the manifestation of Brahman. This state is called Rechaka (exhaling). The subsequent contemplation that "I am that Brahman" is Puraka (inhaling). To continue that contemplation without interruption is Kumbhaka (steady inkeeping of Prana). Such is the nature of Pranayama meant for the wise. To the ignorant it simply means regulation of breath.'[1]

When a man experiences Enlightenment, the texts say, he simultaneously attains to the Siddhis, or spiritual powers. These are, among

[1] Quoted by G. H. Mees, *The Revelation in the Wilderness* (N. Kluwer-Deventer).

others: clairvoyance, remembering past incarnations, levitation, transmutation of the elements, and omniscience.

But what are these powers? They may be psychic powers, yet it is apparent from observing people who apparently exercise these, that a psychically developed person is not necessarily one who is spiritually developed. He is not a Christ or a Buddha.

Yet it is also apparent that an Enlightened man may have psychic powers, not because he has tried to acquire them and has made them an end in themselves, but because they have developed naturally in the course of his spiritual growth.

At the level of total achievement, the Siddhis can mean something far more than psychic power. Clairvoyance at this level means clear vision. Nothing is hidden. Reality is perceived face to face with no veil between. An Enlightened man will see all things as they are, not as they seem to be.

Remembrance of past incarnations is to know Who one has been from the beginning, including all the 'bodies' that have been used as vehicles of the Self.

Levitation can refer to the raising of earth to Heaven, of self to Self, the empirical consciousness to Divine Consciousness, man to God.

To have transmuted the elements means to have transmuted the base metal of self into the gold of Self. What was the work of the Alchemists if it was not the transmutation of man into God? The Self is the True Gold and the Elixir of Life.

Omniscience comes with the experience of the One and the All. It is seeing the Universe as it really is and therefore 'knowing all things'.

All this becomes apparent very slowly and it is only the beginning of understanding. There is always more to be discovered.

As I climb the sevenfold ladder, consciousness is transformed into Consciousness. I accomplish the great Liberation. I recognize the great Serpent Goddess Kundalini to be a symbol of this ascent, as gradually She rises through the seven spheres.

I know I have to follow the path of the great mantra OM MANI PADME HUM.[1] No longer can I believe that the simple repetition of these or any other syllables will spiritualize my being. Rather I have to become the jewel in the lotus.

While I remain unenlightened and the lower self is out of touch with the Higher and the sense-perception consciousness has no knowledge of the Universal Consciousness, there is no experience of the Real, no reflection of the Light. Because of this my action in the world is unspiritual, chaotic, reflecting the chaos within.

[1] This mantra is translated as 'Hail to the Jewel in the Heart of the Lotus!'

Therefore I am told in these teachings that, if I am to understand and help the world, I must understand and help myself. If I wish to know the nature of God, I must find my own True Nature. Then my knowledge will be Self-knowledge instead of the limited fact-knowledge of the intellect. I will have learned how to act compassionately instead of destructively. Good intentions, skill, self-control are not enough. It is only the Enlightened Who can lift mankind nearer to the Light.

The law is to give to the utmost of one's capacity and knowledge at all times, but giving should become not a self-conscious act but a 'pulse of existence'.

What I have to offer is not what I possess but what I am. The extent of my awareness of God is implicit in everything I think, speak, do, and also give. If I am not one with God, my thoughts, speech, action and help are necessarily limited. With the best of intentions, I may only create more suffering than before. If I am still struggling with the manifestations of the lower mind and am not dedicated to Self-realization, I can do great harm in the world, yet imagine that I am doing good. Until I have realized the Atman in myself, I am still dead and asleep. I cannot give the Whole.

If I am to give the Whole, I must become the Whole. So Krishna says in the Bhagavad Gita which describes the way to be followed: 'On Me fix thy mind, give thyself in love to Me; sacrifice to Me; prostrate thyself before Me; having thus united thy whole self with Me as thy Goal, to Me thou shalt come.'

In the symbolic language of earth (sensory perception) I should dig for the hidden treasure; of water (the emotions) I should cross over the river to the further shore; of fire (the lower mind) I should consume what stands in the way of Self-realization; of air (the intuition) I should fly like the eagle towards the Sacred Mountain, God.

While I lie asleep, the Creative Power which is called Kundalini sleeps in the lowest of the seven centres,[1] and cannot begin the work of transmutation. Idleness in the sense of ignorance of and indifference to the spiritual kingdom in myself prevents It from becoming active.

In this state of soul sleep, my desire is for the 'things of this world' which may include great intellectual achievements as well as the usual 'pleasures'. This is the abuse of the Creative Power. If I awake and my desire becomes longing for liberation, for 'the things of heaven', I can use the Creative Power to rise to ever higher levels of consciousness. For Kundalini[2] to awake, I must admit the inadequacy of my

---

[1] The muladhara chakra.
[2] On the path of the Fall, Kundalini, the Creative Power of Consciousness is the Tempter (see Genesis); on the path of the Return, the Liberator.

intellect to answer the questions: Who am I; What is life? I must try intuitively to grasp what there is still to be experienced that would explain all things to me. As I begin to listen to my intuition which gradually reflects more and more light, I will slowly understand how to overcome the illusory self and may begin to experience the Real Self.

This process extends over the first four centres or chakras.

Through how many lifetimes have I lain in this sleep, holding the Self a prisoner?

For how long have I been engaged in the pursuit of happiness in a material sense, in flight from suffering, in search for the physical beloved, intellectual achievement, success and power over others in one form or another? For how long has Energy gone into the effort to possess what I wanted and keep what I already had?

And how many times before I really became aware of it have I seen this kind of existence as one of suffering and ignorance and death but not known how to transform it into life? How often does the same kind of experience have to recur before I can transcend it?

These states of death and the stirring to life are described over and over again by the men who know the Way. There is no phase that is unknown to them, but the predicament is never without a solution.

When therefore I read about the manipura centre or lotus, symbol of the lower mind, I recognize myself. In Hindu teaching, it has ten aspects or petals. These are: shame, fickleness, jealousy, unpurified desire, laziness, sorrow, ignorance, aversion, disgust and fear.

This level of consciousness is called the great battlefield, Kuruk-shetra,[1] where the liberating forces in man fight to the death those that would hold him enslaved. They are the armies of Light and Darkness, Good and Evil, Michael and Lucifer and the battle takes place, not in a mythical sky or historical past or future but within me.

The unpurified lower mind is the hydra-headed monster that has to be slain before I can awake to Eternal Life.

It is this death that is the Great Death in life. It is this Dragon that is slain by the Hero, or hushed to sleep by the one who takes the Pearl.

Sri Rama kills Ravana, Theseus kills the Minotaur, Perseus Medusa, St. George the Dragon.

This Death is the annihilation of ignorance, suffering, illusion and unpurified desire.

To help me transmute the ten petals of the manipura lotus into the rays of the jewelled city, there are ten rules or precepts. There are the ten Yamas and Niyamas of Patanjali, the Ten Qualities and the Ten

---

[1] Bhagavad Gita.

67

Higher Qualities given in the Bhagavad Gita; there are the Ten Pious Acts and Ten Rules of Buddhism.

These teach the way of detachment from the passions of greed, coveting, jealousy, pride, anger and fear. They teach the outer self to become the servant of the Inner and to learn how to hear and obey Its Voice.

The following passage by the eleventh-century Tibetan yogi Milarepa tells how this should be done:

'Within the Temple of the Bodhi Hill, my body, within my breast,
   wherein the Altar is,
Within the chamber topmost and triangular within my heart.
The Horse of Mind, moving like the wind, doth prance about. . . .
To catch the Horse, use, as the Lasso, Singleness of Purpose;
It must be tied, when caught, to the Post of Meditation;
It must be fed, when hungry, with the Guru's Teachings;
It must be given to drink, when thirsty, of the Stream of Consciousness;
It must be kept, when cold, in the Enclosure of the Voidness.
For Saddle, use the Will, for Bridle, Intellect;
Attach to It, as Girths and Cruppers, Fixedness Immoveable;
Around it pass, as Head-stall and as Nose-band, the Vital Airs (Pranas);
Its rider is the Youth of Intellect (Keen Watchfulness);
The Helmet, which he weareth, is Mahayanic Altruism;
His Coat of Mail is Learning, Thought, and Contemplation;
Upon his back he carrieth the Shield of Patience;
He holdeth, in his hand, the long Spear Aspiration;
And, by his side, hangeth the Sword, Intelligence; . . .
This Horse doth course along the wide-spread Plain of Happiness;
Its goal is the attainment of the State of all the Conquerors (Buddhas).
Its Hind-part leaveth, in its rear, attachment to Samsaric life;
Its Front-part goeth on to the safe place of Deliverance.
By running such a race, I'm carried on to Buddhahood;
Judge if this be like your own conception of felicity:
Worldly Happiness I covet not.'[1]

This work cannot be done without love. If the Atman is not the Beloved, I cannot grow towards It, for there is no other force strong enough to bring me to It. If there is no part of me that believes It exists, none that knows that Union is possible, none that will humble itself enough to admit that at present I am a drop in comparison with

[1] From *Tibet's Great Yoga Milarepa* by the Lama Kazi Dawa-Sandup and Dr W. Y. Evans-Wentz (O.U.P.).

an ocean, none that will accept the guidance of those who are already Enlightened, the work will be impossible.

If there is love of Truth and Light, all the rest will follow. So Krishna says in the Bhagavad Gita: 'Neither by (study of) the Vedas, nor by austerities, nor by sacrifice can I be seen as thou hast seen Me; but by single-hearted devotion alone can I be known in this Form, O Arjuna, and perceived in Essence and also entered into.'[1]

This process is like the growth of a lotus which as a seed in earth desires to reach the sun. It rises through mud and water into air until at last, in response to the warmth of the sun, it flowers.

Again, Krishna says:

'Giving the self in love to Me, with Me as Goal, doing all actions for Me (the One Life in all) devoid of all attachment to the forms, free from hostility to any being, man comes to Me, O Arjuna.'[1]

As this work proceeds the nature of Reality will be experienced ever more completely and I will say with Arjuna, 'Thou art the Knower, the One to be known and the Supreme Abode. By Thee alone this Universe is pervaded . . . overjoyed am I to see what I have never seen before.'

Hinduism and Buddhism teach that until I begin to awake and do this work, I am subject to the law which is called Karma in the East, and Fate in the West. 'As the Persian Wheel in drawing water from a well goes up and down, moved by the bullocks, so the soul passes through life, moved by its deeds,' says an ancient text.[2]

It is the unpurified lower self and its actions that impel me to rebirth. I am a slave to my lower self until I begin to realize this. The moment that I awake to the existence of the True Self and become aware that my actions can either hold me to earth or lead me to Heaven, I will cease to be the blind instrument of Fate. I will cease to move around the circumference of myself. As I move towards the centre, so will my actions reflect a greater degree of Self-awareness. I will have a direction instead of acting 'blindly'. All the searches – for power, love, knowledge – become the one search of which all the others were but the pale reflection. As the one search leads me towards the Self, so I will free this True Nature from the 'elements' that hid It. When this work is complete and I am united with God, Karma or the law of cause and effect no longer exists. It is transcended, because cause and effect are one.

As I work I will realize with astonshiment that it is not I who am

[1] From *The Yoga of the Bhagavad Gita*, by Sri Krishna Prem (Watkins).
[2] From the Gheranda Samhita, quoted by G. H. Mees in *The Revelation in the Wilderness* (N. Kluwer-Deventer).

acting but the Self. I, the lower, unpurified mind and the body, am that Self.

I only think of myself as separate from God because I do not feel, think and know that everything I am is God. That is why, in the East, the world I perceive while in this state of ignorance is called illusion. If I can only awake, it will no longer be illusion. I will see it as myself and as God. I will be it and God.

They say further that what reincarnates is the effects of the causes engendered by the mind separate from God. What I am and do in this life will result in the person I am in the next, with all the circumstances of birth, environment, character, handicaps and abilities, etc. that are involved. This person that I am now or the one that I have been or will be is the vehicle of the Self, is the Self, although I have not always known it. Life after life I may have lived in darkness and ignorance of Who I am until the suffering and agony engendered by my own actions force me to wake up. If I can maintain this awareness I will attract to myself the experiences which will cause it to grow further. What comes to me as the circumstances of life comes as the effects of what I do and in response to what I ask for. I continue the work in my next life at the point where it is broken off until the end is reached and my destiny achieved.

Once the process of the Fall is reversed into the Return, the temptations formerly succumbed to are put to me again as tests. Each difficult situation in life becomes a blessing instead of a curse because it gives me the opportunity of coming nearer to the Self, of learning how to co-operate with Its Will.

Its Will as I now know is to become Whole, not to remain separated into fragments. In prolonging the fragmentation, I only draw down upon myself sorrow and suffering. Desiring to help the Self to become One, I shorten the time of my wandering in Samsara or the wilderness. I may continue to suffer as long as I am separate, but at least I know why I am suffering and that there will be an end to it.

I know that I will one day be able to say with the Buddha: 'Now art thou seen, O Builder. Never again shalt thou build house for me. Broken are the beams and sundered lies the ridge-pole. My mind is set on the Eternal, Extinguished is all desire.' There will be no desire because I am what I am. There is no further need to become.

If I understand this teaching of what I am, I can begin to walk the Noble Eightfold Path laid down by the Buddha. If I accept the Four Noble Truths of suffering, the cause of suffering, its overcoming and the way that leads to its overcoming, then from this attitude will grow, in time, the other seven stages:

perfect aspirations
perfect speech
perfect action
perfect livelihood
perfect effort
perfect mindfulness
perfect concentration

Perfect in this context means complete or single-minded.[1] The cause of suffering is separation from God and earth-bound desire. The way to its overcoming is the transmutation of desire into the longing for Liberation.

For guidance I have the Voice of the Hidden Self, reflected at first in the intuition ever leading me to It through the practice of self-surrender in the experiences of life. My teacher in the outer world, if I have one, or several, will simply reflect this Voice. Different teachers may be needed for different stages of the path. Personal experience may be the only teacher for long periods. As for how to look for one, the saying is: 'When the man is ready, the teacher appears.' There is no need to comb the earth looking for one. Life will lead me to the right place at the right time if I will but surrender to its guidance and not try to arrange things as I want them. Let me realize what the work is, and at once the Self will become the Friend instead of the Enemy. I can no longer blame It[2] for the suffering It causes me but will recognize that the cause of suffering lies in myself and that in myself is the way to overcome it. Then I welcome what life brings, will learn to surrender what I want or do not want to happen to what does happen. Each experience will bring me closer to the Self. In accepting life, I recognize and accept Its guidance. I recognize Who is at work and give thanks, even for suffering.

I realize as I read the texts for inspiration or guidance that my work is to transform the manipura lotus into the jewelled city; to move from sensory to intuitive perception of the world and myself, from fire to air; will I continue to veil the Source or will I work in such a way that the veils can be dissolved? 'The phenomenal world is unreal,' I say at this twilight stage. But it is only unreal because I have not experienced the Real; I do not see it as God but as the world. When, like all the heroes, I have withdrawn the sword from the scabbard and it flashes through the seven spheres, I will see it as God.

As I learn slowly how to do this, I can observe the effects of the

[1] See the Lama Govinda's *Foundations of Tibetan Mysticism* (Rider), where he uses this word instead of the word 'right'.
[2] Calling It God, Fate or Life, in the sense of Powers outside of me.

freeing of light upon my emotional life that becomes more balanced, upon my intellectual concepts that change and develop; on my relations with the world that are quite altered, even on my physical body. As I work in consciousness of the Light, knowing that I am the darkness shrouding It, so It begins to shine and I can see clearly what still blocks Its Radiance. With ever-growing love I dig in the earth to release the Prisoner, knowing that He is myself and that He is slowly transforming my being from base metal into gold.

II

If this is the essence of Hinduism and Buddhism and I have been too blind to see it until now, how much more is there to be discovered?

If I turn now to the West, what can I find? Need I still reject Christianity? Behind the degenerate outer forms which are the stones I have stumbled over, there may still be bread.

How many centuries, how many lives has it taken me to realize that beyond a certain level I am neither Christian nor Hindu, nor Buddhist, nor Muslim, nor Jew? I am simply man, trying to unite his finite self with Infinite Being.

And if now I stand in all the churches of Europe, Catholic and Protestant, longing to cut away the dead wood and allow the tree of life to grow, can I answer the question 'What is the meaning of Christianity'?

What does the Bible say? What did Christ teach? What is the meaning of the Crucifixion and the Resurrection? For how long have I been as Nicodemus was two thousand years ago – unable to grasp the meaning of the Law?

'There was a man of the Pharisees, named Nicodemus, a ruler of the Jews: the same came to Jesus by night and said unto him, Rabbi, we know that thou art a teacher come from God: for no man can do these miracles that thou doest, except God be with him.

'Jesus answered and said unto him: Verily, verily I say unto thee, except a man be born again, he cannot see the Kingdom of God.

'Nicodemus saith unto him: How can a man be born when he is old? Can he enter a second time into his mother's womb, and be born?

'Jesus answered, verily, verily, I say unto thee, Except a man be born of water and of the Spirit, he cannot enter into the Kingdom of God.

'That which is born of the flesh is flesh; and that which is born of the Spirit is spirit.

'Marvel not that I say unto thee, Ye must be born again.

'The wind bloweth where it listeth, and thou hearest the sound thereof but canst not tell whence it cometh, and whither it goeth; so is everyone that is born of the Spirit.

'Nicodemus answered and said unto him, How can these things be?

'Jesus answered and said unto him, Art thou a master of Israel and knowest not these things?'[1]

There is a Mahayana hymn to the Enlightened Ones:

> All the Buddhas are wonderful and glorious.
> There is not their equal upon earth.
> They reveal to us the Path of Life.
> And we hail their appearance with pious reverence.
> All the Buddhas teach the same truth,
> The truth points out the Way to those
> Who have gone wrong.
> The truth is our hope and comfort
> We gratefully accept its illimitable Light.
> All the Buddhas are one in Essence,
> Which is omnipresent in all modes of being,
> Sanctifying the bonds that tie all souls together
> And we rest in its bliss as our Final Refuge.'[2]

Can I who am a Christian accept this statement? Can I accept the fact that all the Buddhas, including Christ, are Sons of God? Can I who am a Christian also be a Buddhist, a Hindu, a Taoist? Can I follow the Buddhas because I am man and wish to become Man?

I can if I understand the teaching of the Virgin Birth to mean the birth of man in God and God in man, during my life on earth. Then I am no different from the Yogi who works to be reborn in Brahman or the Buddhist who seeks the experience of Nirvana, or the Taoist to be one with the Tao. All tread the same path and all follow the same God – their own True Self.

If I use the key, I can interpret the Christian doctrine to mean that this Self, the Father, God, is with all men. Man has only to know he is the Son. He has only to become what he IS. The clue is here. In order to be and to know, one has to become.

If I can accept this, so much becomes clear.

The Christian version of the Creation of the Universe and the Fall of Man is no longer an historical account of the origin of the physical universe but an allegorical description of the Spiritual Path; of man's separation from and return to God.

[1] Gospel of St. John 3: 1-10.
[2] Quoted by G. H. Mees, *The Revelation in the Wilderness* (N. Kluwer-Deventer).

God is not a superior person made in my own image – the idol He has degenerated into – but my True Self. He is not accessible to my intellect which cannot comprehend Him. He is 'outside time and space', beyond the pairs of opposites of 'this world', the fallen consciousness. Like Brahman in Hinduism or the Tao in Taoism He can only be experienced in the 'now' of intuitive insight into His Nature.

In the Old Testament, He is the Enemy, constantly chastising the Children of Israel because they do not follow His Commandments, yet promising them the 'inheritance of the earth' if they do.

To those who listen to Him and do His Commandments, He is the Friend. Moses, Solomon, David, Daniel, for example, love rather than fear Him. The Prophets 'hear His Voice'.

In the New Testament He is the Loving Father Who sends His Son to save the world. 'The Father loveth the Son, and sheweth him all things that himself doeth.'[1]

What is written in the Bible refers to the life of every man. God is terrifying when He is the Enemy and the Unknown. He sends disaster after disaster until He is recognized. There seems no end to suffering; no point to existence; no rest for the weary; no bread for the hungry.

Once He is recognized and loved, He is no longer frightening. He is the Helper, guiding the soul to Himself, drawing it closer to His Radiance. The wandering in the wilderness then becomes the preparation for entry into the Promised Land.

The Promised Land in the New Testament is the Kingdom of Heaven and Jesus-Christ, the Son of God, is the Saviour Who teaches the Way to the Father. Because He is one with the Father, He speaks as the Father: 'I am the way, the truth and the life.'[2] 'I am the resurrection and the life.'[3] 'Before Abraham was, I am.'[4]

Jesus is the Saviour because He is man who has become one with God. He is the Way for other men to follow. Despite his human parentage, he is able to 'overcome the world' and become the Son.

Christian dogma says that the Godhead has been incarnate in one man only – the historical Jesus. The logical conclusion of this is that the Godhead cannot be incarnate in other men. Yet, unless I realize that the Godhead is incarnate in every single man and my work is to recognize and identify myself with It, I cannot begin to understand the teaching of Jesus.

If I deny the human parentage of Jesus and confuse his human and ordinary birth with his Divine Birth (the Virgin or Second Birth) as the Christ I deprive His teaching of its most important message.

[1] The Gospel of St. John 5:20.   [2] Gospel of St. John 14:6.
[3] Gospel of St. John 11:25.   [4] Gospel of St. John 8:58.

74

If Jesus was a man born of the human race in the usual way who had developed and perfected Himself to the extent that He could 'receive' or 'enter into' God, where God could 'descend' upon and 'transfigure' Him, making Him a Christ, or Anointed One, then the whole Christian doctrine is at once brought into focus with the other great religions.

Then it is perfectly clear why 'no man cometh unto the Father but by me'. No man can understand What and Who the Father is, unless he follows the way of the Son which is the way to Christhood. I cannot know the Father until I have become a Christ.

The Buddha also had a 'Virgin Birth' but this again refers to His birth into 'Buddha-Consciousness' and not to His physical birth. As with the life of Jesus the story of the Buddha's life is such a closely woven tapestry of the eternal traditions of spiritual rebirth and of the events of the earth-lives of the men who achieved it, that if I have not the key, it is impossible to disentangle one from the other. When Jesus speaks as the True Self, for example, every word is from the Father. Every action is the Father's Will. This is illustrated by His answer to Philip[1]: 'Philip saith unto him, Lord, shew us the Father, and it sufficeth us. Jesus saith unto him, Have I been so long time with you and yet hast thou not known me, Philip? He that hath seen me hath seen the Father; and how sayest thou then, shew us the Father? Believest thou not that I am in the Father and the Father in me? the words that I speak unto you I speak not of myself: but the Father that dwelleth in me, he doeth the works.'

If I can interpret Christianity as being the teaching of how man can return to the Father in life and not in a future after-death heaven, what light does this shed on the fundamental doctrine?

Heaven is then not everlasting (in the sense of duration of time) life in a Paradise conceived by the mind of man, but is eternally existent. I have only to 'find it'. It is the experience of oneness with God.

Hell is the life of the unenlightened, the dead. It is existence separate from God. It is therefore not a place of horror conceived of by man's tormented imagination where all those who have 'done evil' in this life will go after death and suffer everlasting damnation. It is the desire-bound existence that I have called life.

In the Bible, Christ descends into hell to 'save sinners'.

If I understand that Christ is a synonym for God or the True Self, then it is clear that His descent is one into His own nature in order to transmute and raise it to oneness with Himself.

In order that I may 'receive' the descent of my God-nature, I must

[1] Gospel of St. John, 14:8-10.

75

know Who I am and prepare for Its Coming by the work of self-purification.

I must enter the dark unknown called by psychologists the 'subconscious' or the 'unconscious', the labyrinth of the inner world of my mind.[1]

If I follow Ariadne's thread, the way out of it will be found. Paradoxically, the way out is the way into myself. The deeper I go, the more I realize Who I am. I know myself and at the same time discover God. In the process of becoming God, my lower nature is redeemed because it is illumined slowly by His descent. This process may be called perhaps, 'the passing through Purgatory'.

Then indeed Hell is transfigured into Heaven.

The Fall of man, like the Hindu Fall, is not a historical event but is the state of every man who is separated from his True Self and is not treading the path of Return.

Lucifer is the symbol of the fallen man. Yet his name means 'Light-bearer'. Though fallen from God-consciousness, I am nevertheless the Light-bearer. I am ignorant of my True Nature, yet It is within me. 'The light shineth in darkness; and the darkness comprehended it not.'[2] I have only to acknowledge the Light in order eventually to become the Light. In the first chapter of the Gospel of St. John, there are the words: 'He (John) was not that Light (was not one with It) but was sent to bear witness of that Light. That was the true Light (God), which lighteth every man that cometh into the world. He (God) was in the world (the lower Luciferic nature), and the world was made by him, and the world knew him not. He came unto his own, and his own received him not. But as many as received him, to them he gave power to become the Sons of God, even to them that believe on his name: which were born, not of blood, nor of the will of the flesh, nor of the will of man, but of God.'[3]

Lucifer is the 'world' that 'knew him not'. He is myself in whom God is veiled, disguised, hidden. The man in whom God is 'revealed', who 'receives' Him, is a Christ, or one 'Anointed by God'.

Fallen, Luciferic man lives in sin because he commits the fundamental sin of being separate from God. God is not his Father. Therefore, Jesus says to the Pharisees: 'If God were your Father, ye would love me . . . why do you not understand my speech? even because ye cannot hear my word. Ye are of your father the devil,[4] and the lusts of your father ye will do. He was a murderer (of the True Self) from the

---

[1] For the best interpretation of this subject in psychological terms, see the works of C. G. Jung.
[2] Gospel of St. John 1:5.   [3] Verses 8-13.   [4] The devil is the lower self.

76

beginning, and abode not in the truth, because there is no truth in him . . . He that is of God heareth God's words; ye therefore hear them not, because ye are not of God.'[1]

My fundamental sin has been ignorance of my separation from God. To sin means to miss the mark.[2] The mark is God. If I am separate I appropriate to myself what belongs to God. All the other sins of pride, coveting, jealousy, anger, sloth, result from this primal one. The sin of 'killing' the Light results in killing at every level including the physical one where it becomes the killing of men who are literally my Self since all are Light-bearers. If I were a true Christian, a Christed one, it would be impossible for me to kill, I would know that all men are myself and that in killing them, at whatever level, I kill myself.

The desire to possess is the characteristic of fallen man. I want what is not mine but can only be called God's and, living in this illusion, I covet what belongs to others. When I have returned to God, am one with Him, I can no longer commit these sins. I 'want' nothing because I am everything. The primal sin and therefore all the others are wiped out by oneness-with-God.

The act of Liberation when a man becomes a Son of God lifts all mankind a little nearer to the Light but it cannot take away other men's sin. If the sins of humanity had been taken away by Christ there would be no hell but only Paradise on earth. Yet in the 'eternal' sense, it is true to say that Christ takes away the sins of the world, because when a man becomes a Christ, his sins are absolved. I have to accomplish this for myself. No-one can do it for me. I must redeem my own world and become my own Saviour.

Salvation is at-one-ment with the True Self. God will 'save the world' when I have overcome the world and am reborn in Him. The only salvation is the final rest of the Seventh Day – which does not take place in the 'future' but at the moment when past and future are transcended in the permanent experience of the now, the eternally present Reality of God.[3] If I can only break my death-like sleep and awake to what I am, I will ultimately know the rest of the Sabbath.

How many in the past have realized this? Now I can understand the words of Boehme that puzzled me years ago, and those of Nicolas of Cusa:

[1] Gospel of St. John 8:42-47.
[2] For a full analysis of this interpretation, see *The Mark*, by Maurice Nicoll (Vincent Stuart Ltd).
[3] The glimpses of Reality experienced in the course of the Return are not the Seventh Day but only a foretaste of It. Therefore it says in the Tibetan Precepts of the Gurus: 'A mere glimpse of Reality may be mistaken for complete Realization.'

'In all faces is shown the Face of faces, veiled and in a riddle. Howbeit unveiled it is not seen, until, above all faces, a man enter into a certain secret and mystic silence, where there is no knowing or concept of a face. This mist, cloud, darkness or ignorance into which he that seeketh Thy Face entereth, when he goeth beyond all knowledge or concept, is the state below which Thy Face cannot be found, except veiled; but that very darkness revealeth Thy Face to be there beyond all veils. Hence I observe how needful it is for me to enter into the darkness and to admit the coincidence of opposites, beyond all grasp of reason, and there to seek the Truth, where Impossibility meeteth us.'[1]

If I do not seek this experience beyond the grasp of what I am at present, I will remain dead, though I am called alive.

It is clear now that the Sabbath is no different from the rest of the serpent power Kundalini, the Great Goddess who having climbed up through the six levels of being and dissolved the six veils, returns whence She came and reaches the seventh where She is united with the Supreme Lord in the Bliss of At-one-ment. It is She who then becomes the Queen of Heaven.[2]

It is to the Seventh Day that these words apply: 'Everything that is not before thy face and that which is hidden from thee shall be revealed to thee. For there is nothing hidden that shall not be made manifest, nor buried which shall not be raised.'[3]

On the Seventh Day, I become both the Son of Man and the Son of God. I reach true Manhood by becoming one with God.

I have lived the threefold path taught by the Tradition; the Path of Purification, Illumination and Union.

To this Seventh Day belongs the Resurrection when I am born of the Spirit into full experience of the Light.

How shall I come to the experience of the Resurrection?

'Let not him who seeketh cease until he findeth and when he findeth he shall wonder; and wondering he shall reign, and reigning he shall rest.'[4]

If a man seeks the Father, the Father will come to Him.

The rituals of Christianity as well as the Bible can be of help now because they have come alive for me.

How shall I understand the sacraments?

Can I see them now as reflections of the True Sacraments which are the revelation of God in man? The ceremony of baptism for example

[1] Nicolas of Cusa.
[2] In the Christian tradition this return is called the Assumption of the Virgin.
[3] From the Gnostic 'Sayings of Jesus'. See also Gospel of St. Luke 8:17.
[4] From the Gnostic 'Sayings of Jesus' in G. R. S. Mead, *Fragments of a Faith Forgotten* (Watkins).

is a symbol of what the True Baptism is. It confers no grace in itself yet I can learn from it. My work cannot be done for me by any external means, nor can God work through the external church, however much it is said to derive from His authority; He works within me only. The Grace He confers is in response to my aspiration, longing and work for it. Baptism is a tremendous Initiation into the Nature of God. It is not something automatically conferred on me by a priest, making me into a Christian. No grace imparted through the church can make me a Christian. Only I, with the help of God, can make myself one.

As with baptism, so with the other sacraments. A child is confirmed as he is baptized without having the slightest idea of Who or What God is, Who or What he is himself or how he should go about discovering either. He learns the catechism by heart, goes through a ceremony which permits him henceforth to take Communion. But with Whom is he communing? Does he know? Intuitively he may 'feel' what Communion means but unless he knows what it means, how can he recognize the symbolic nature of the act he is performing?

Again, what does the changing of the bread and wine on the altar into the body and blood of Christ by the sacrament of the Holy Eucharist mean?

What is the true miracle of Transubstantiation? Is it not the transmutation of man into God? When I take the bread and the wine, am I not 'eating' and 'drinking' what I can become, and, in fact, Am? It is *my* sacrifice that is required to redeem the sins of *my* world. It is useless to perpetuate the memory of Christ's Sacrifice if I do not understand its meaning. If I know that I am to follow the way of Jesus-Christ and like him transform the bread and wine of my being into the 'body and blood' of a Christ, then it is worth while participating consciously in the Mass. If not, the ceremony is simply superstition, literally – 'what is left over' after the Spirit has gone and only the letter remains.

The sacrament of penance is of psychological benefit but has it no deeper meaning? Why should I ask a priest for the absolution that only God can give? What is repentance other than the 'turning around'[1] within and the realization of the sacrifice required if God's will is to be done and Earth to become Heaven. When Earth is Heaven, there will be complete absolution for all 'sins'. As I repent I learn how to serve the one instead of the many and so purify the levels of my being, that I begin to see God.

If I interpret the sacrament of marriage in the same way, as a symbol of the Mystic Marriage between man and God, or between the risen

[1] Metanoia.

and purified Consciousness and its Source, then it becomes of tremendous significance. Earthly marriage is the reflection of the Mystic Marriage and can often guide a person closer to it. Formerly, and perhaps even now in some cases, Hinduism taught the bride to look upon her husband as the Lord of the Universe, and her True Self. Similarly the husband recognized the Divine Mother and Queen of Heaven in his wife. By this method, both were taught to overcome the difficulties of marriage and transmute it into the perfect union, symbol of the Great Union of man and God, of Siva and Parvati, or Siva and Sakti which in all traditions is the prerequisite of the Second Birth.

Finally, the sacrament of extreme unction becomes a symbol of the 'Anointing' which transforms man into the Son of Man and the Son of God. It takes place at the death of the physical body, which itself is the symbol of the Great Death in Life. When the top of the head, traditionally associated with the seventh plane of consciousness, is anointed by God the sahasrara padma bursts into flower and man becomes a Christ. Then takes place the true Holy Communion of which the sacrament of the Eucharist is the symbol only.

If I question further, there are more answers.

Advent becomes the time of waiting for the birth in myself of the Christ nature. In the cycle of the year the winter solstice is the time when the sun is 'born' and begins its ascent into the mid-heaven.

Advent covers the whole period of waiting for release from the prison of the Fall by this Divine Birth. It extends over lifetimes. The first manifestation of it is the dim perception that the Light exists, distant and veiled but nevertheless casting a faint glimmer upon the path. Hesitantly I begin to walk towards it; often doubting that it exists; often losing sight of it, yet growing more sure that I must find it: each year, as I proceed, a little more Light is born in the cave of my heart. Each year I am more aware that Advent announces the Birth and that the Birth is taking place within me. Only by 'confession' of the sin of separateness from God can I begin to 'be converted', to turn around in myself and face the Light. I know that only by waiting for, watching and loving the Light, can I experience the Blessing of the Millennium which is to become the Light.

Little by little, as I follow the solar path into the highest heaven, I experience in myself the Virgin Birth of the Divine Nature. I begin to 'see' Who I am. Step by step, my fallen self is transmuted into the Radiant Adamantine Nature of all the Liberated Ones and I uncover the Treasure that is buried in earth.

Christmas is celebrated at the time of year when the sun is most 'hidden'. How often have I remembered the birth of the Son of God, little knowing that the Christ-nature can be born in me also, that I also, if I will 'receive It', can become a Son of God? 'But as many as received him, even to them he gave the power to become the Sons of God.' How often have I read these words and not applied them to myself?

After the birth of God-consciousness in man, there is Baptism.

In the early church (pre-third century) and in the Albigensian rituals in the thirteenth century, there was no infant baptism. It was a ceremony of the utmost solemnity and significance, attended only by men prepared for Self-realization, in whom the 'child' had long been born. On receiving Baptism, a man was said to 'rise from the dead' and 'never to grow old' which means that he had seen his True Nature face to face.

It was only after His Baptism that Jesus began his mission in the world. It is not the ceremony that can transform the dead into the Living but the actual experience of the Father.

As it was with Him so it can be with other men, when, perfectly constituted in their lower selves, purified after having bathed mind and emotions and intuition in the Living Waters of Truth, they experience for the first time full consciousness of their Spiritual Nature. Like a flash of lightning on the physical plane, a direct channel of communication is opened with that Nature and it is realized that 'I and my Father are one'. This is the descent of the Dove, the Holy Spirit upon the man able to receive and recognize It. Upon such a nature It works a further transformation until that man can 'return to his Father' and experience the final stage of the birth, or the Resurrection of the Seventh Day.

What is the difference between Baptism and Resurrection? Is it perhaps that the first is the partial experience of the Father giving man experience of the truth that he is the Son, and the second the complete experience, the final ascent to the Father? Baptism follows the purification and harmonizing of the four lower elements[1] in man and is the direct communication with the fifth, ether, the Quintessence, the True Self. But before the greater experience of the Seventh Heaven at the moment of Resurrection, there is the temptation and the Death.

Jesus was tempted by the Devil[2] for forty days after the Baptism – during which time he did not touch the food of 'this world' – meaning that he did not forget Who he was and fall again. Unlike Lot's wife, who was turned to a pillar of salt, he did not look back.

These temptations are put at different stages of the path to every man who is in search of God. They were put to Jesus and the Buddha.

[1] Earth, water, fire and air.   [2] Ahankara, the lower self.

The devil who tempts is not some 'creature of the imagination' but the lower self which in Hinduism is called Ahankara and in Buddhism Mara. It is the will of the lower self which is forever trying to oppose the Will of God and it is this that must be annihilated before the Will of God can be done.

Therefore it happens that before the Resurrection there is the Death.

In order for me to become, like Jesus, a 'Saviour of Being', I must recognise what has 'killed' that Being.

What is the meaning of the Crucifixion?

Is the death on the cross the same Death that is spoken of in the literature of other religions? Does it symbolize the giving up of all in the lower self that stands in the way of Union? Is it the final extinction of desire? To make my will become that of the Father so that both work for Union means that I must give up all the petty and separate wills that want other things. It is they that interfere with communion between us.

Acceptance and surrender are carried through to the end of the world. The last desire is the desire for help and the cry 'My God, my God, why hast thou forsaken me?' Even this is overcome by the acceptance of the way through the agony: 'Lord, into Thy hands I commend my spirit.'

To die in the personal will is to allow the Will of the Father, the True Nature to act. It is this gradual dying that allows the birth of the Light in darkness and the slow ascent into Heaven. Realization may come in a flash, but the preparation for it is long and arduous.

The crucifixion of Jesus symbolizes both the crucifixion of the God-Nature by the lower nature, and the death of that lower nature. God is crucified by the 'world' – the blind self in me that cannot recognize or admit His existence. On the path of the Return, God is freed from the cross and the lower self takes His place. If the crucifixion of God is to end, I must awake from my sleep and transform the Tree of Death (the cross) into the Tree of Life. I must, like Jesus, become the Saviour of Being, the Saviour of God and of myself. I suffer because I have shut up God in the cave of my heart and have hidden His Light. I become triumphant as gradually, by dying to myself, that Light which is the awareness of God is born in my soul. It is only the veils of the lower levels of consciousness that prevent me from knowing that God is myself. The tearing of the veils can only be achieved by sacrifice of the false conception of Reality and all that goes with it – all the personal 'I's that struggle to uphold and perpetuate the illusion of separateness. By making this sacrifice, the other Great Sacrifice of God, the Lamb slain from the beginning of the World, is redeemed. By that death and by that redemption man truly becomes a Christ. His True Nature shines forth. In that Nature is no longer Judas, the Betrayer, symbol of the fallen self – the 'son of perdition'.

In the Revelation of St. John the Divine, there are these words: 'And I beheld, and lo, in the midst of the throne and of the four beasts,[1] and in the midst of the elders, stood a lamb as it had been slain, having seven horns and seven eyes, which are the seven Spirits of God sent forth into all the earth.'

When I have redeemed the sacrifice of the Lamb by uniting the seven fragments of His being, I will have 'seven horns and seven eyes, which are the seven Spirits of God'. I will have loosed the seven seals of the Book, penetrated the seven veils, climbed the sevenfold ladder and known the bliss of the Seventh Day.

'He that overcometh shall inherit all things, and I will be his God, and he shall be my son.'

The work of penetrating the veils hiding God is seen at first as 'my' work, 'my' effort, but as it proceeds, I realize that everything is done by God; I have only to respond to His Voice calling from the plane of ether,[2] guiding me to Himself through earth and water and fire and air. As I proceed with the work of sacrifice and transmutation, so is my nature 'changed back' into what it was. The beast becomes the Prince. Ultimately when I have become a Christ, I have saved myself and God and become what during the Fall I had forgotten I am.

To the man who has re-membered Himself, these words apply:

'Though he be a man in the world, yet is he higher than the whole region of the Treasure and shall be exalted above the whole of it.

'Though he be a man in the world, yet shall he be King with me in my Kingdom; He is a man in the world, but a King in the Light.

'Though he be a man in the world, yet is he a man who is not of the world.

'Amen I say unto you; that man is Myself and I am that man.'[3]

Those who are one with Christ in His Kingdom have become Christs also. They are the Community of Saints, the Liberated ones; the Great Avatars. Of all races and times, they are the Sons of God.

No longer can I think of the Crucifixion without realizing that I too will die and be reborn if I follow the Way of Christ.

How many Pilates are there within me, washing their hands of responsibility; how many executioners, wounding by word and deed;

---

[1] The symbols of the four elements.
[2] The plane of direct insight into the Nature of God.
[3] Jesus to his disciples in the Gnostic 'Pistis Sophia'.

how many Marys, agonized spectators of what happens; how many betrayers; how many saviours?

And in the world in which I live and try to come closer to Love, how many are crucified daily by the blind and the ignorant; how many made desolate by the uncontrolled passions of those who continually crucify God and, with God, themselves?

Love cries to me to awake from the tomb where I lie as one dead. Wisdom asks me to resurrect myself and ascend into Heaven, to return to the Father, to know myself.

Religion in the West speaks to me through the symbolism of the death on the Cross and the Resurrection. Religion in the East uses different symbols, yet in them I see the same Teaching.

The limitations of my interpretation of these traditions are the limitations of my vision. I see as far as I can at the moment, yet this is only the beginning of sight.

I am still blind and deaf to the Mystery of God, yet I know that the eyes of the blind can be opened and the ears of the deaf can hear.

Part Six

ALL OVER THE WORLD THE SYMBOLISM IS SCATTERED;
sometimes hidden; sometimes, like the days of the week, so obvious
that it seems fantastic that one has never seen it before. It can be found
in Europe, Africa, Asia, America – anywhere on the face of the earth
that man is. It is in the most exalted philosophies as well as the habits
of everyday life, in the most civilized as well as the most primitive
societies. It is woven into the very tissue of life. One has only to look
and one will find.

It is not beyond the capacity of man to understand it and learn how
to apply it to himself and the enormous problems that face him today.
There is nothing he cannot accomplish if he chooses to obey the Law
of Love.

To comprehend the Infinite, he must become the Infinite.

★   ★   ★   ★

Of the second journey to Asia, only the essence of this symbolism
remains to guide, strengthen and inspire.

I

In Japan I saw many paintings but in front of one I stood astounded.[1]
Others I had admired for their beauty or their mastery of technique,
but none had made my skin prickle and my eyes fill with tears. This
was so powerful that it struck me like a blow.

Who was Sesshu of whom I had never heard? How had he come to
paint like this?

I was told that the philosophy that had formed him, both man and
artist, was Zen.

He never used gold and only seldom colour. Most of his work was
done with black ink and appears to be the expression of an idea worked
out in minutest detail in the mind and then literally thrown on paper
– almost in one stroke.

So it is that a glimpse of Reality is obtained after years of patient

---

[1] Sesshu's winter landscape in the Ueno Museum, Tokyo.

85

work upon the self, in the sudden flash of insight which for that instant unifies all Creation in the experience of Being.

Painting was considered by the Zen Masters to be part of the work of purifying mind and emotions and was an infallible guide to the extent of a man's awareness. It reflected the degree to which he was able to 'go beyond himself'.

It was a method of learning through observation and developed awareness that all phenomena are of one and the same essence, that all are united in the fact of Being. As an artist reached beyond conceptual thought into the experience of the Here and the Now, so he could express in his work the Real that is veiled only by man's faulty perception of it.

The Zen Buddhism which flourished in China from the sixth century onwards and took root in Japan in the thirteenth was not a new teaching but rather a necessary simplification of the one Tradition. In the same way, Buddhism and Christianity were restatements of the original Teaching, which had gradually degenerated into what it was not. All teach the way to awake to Eternal Life in the midst of the everyday life of the world.

Zen Masters define the teaching of Zen in the form of parables. It is for the questioner to discover their meaning. They will not tell him.

Zen apparently has no concepts like Good and Evil, God and the Devil, Nirvana and Samsara, yet its method leads to satori or insight into and identification with the True Self in every man.

For the Enlightened, concepts no longer exist. He has gone beyond them.

From the point of view of the unenlightened, it is a waste of time to cling to them. Concepts will not lead me to the experience of Who I am. The nature of the True Self cannot be taught, described or defined.

In the teaching of Zen, or any other expression of the Tradition, I am either asleep or Awake. If I am asleep my work is to learn how to go beyond the concepts and passions that hold me in trance. If I am Awake, I am Free, Perfect, Whole. While I am asleep I cannot speak of God because I do not know What He Is. If I am Awake, there is no need to speak about God. I am God.

Those who know do not speak.
Those who speak do not know.

The life of Sesshu is one of the best illustrations of what Zen is and how it works. The legend of how he came to choose his name reveals the nature of his life-work.

The word Sesshu means snow-boat.

86

It is related that one day he came across two big Chinese characters written by an ancient sage. He asked a Zen priest their meaning and was told the following story[1]:

'Snow is something that covers the whole world. It is like a jewelled urn which is pure inside and out and shows no speck of dust.

'There is also a boat that floats upon water, ceaselessly moving, now south, now north, now east, now west, without restraint or aim. When these are compared with the human heart, you will see that the snow which is pure and unsullied, represents the heart in the state of absolute serenity. The boat, incessantly in motion, symbolizes the varying changes of the undisciplined heart.

'Go then, and give yourself to meditation, and when you have mastered this in your heart, command your brush to paint. You will see that your painting will improve. Someday people will come to you and say, "Your paintings are heart pictures – of divine and mystical character."

'If anyone should find fault with this interpretation, confidently disregard him. Summer insects should not talk of ice. . . .'

Sesshu was born in 1420, a contemporary of the courageous Portuguese explorers who were shortly to open the eyes of Europe to the wonders of the East. Japan at that time knew only of China and, more remotely, of India. To China she had turned for constant inspiration in art and religion, and in the fifteenth century her scholars and artists experienced a second tremendous wave of Chinese influence in the form of Zen Buddhism. From 1200 onwards, this severe discipline, which had taken form in China, found its way into the monasteries of Japan, brought by visiting monks.

At the age of eleven, Sesshu went to live as a novice in a Zen monastery. At twenty, he moved to the great Shokoku-ji temple at Kyoto, which at that time was the capital of Japan. Here he was able to learn the Chinese language and to have access to a superb collection of Chinese art. There were many paintings by the great masters of the Sung and the Yuan dynasties and these he was able to study in the closest detail under the guidance of a Japanese master-painter called Shubun.

When he felt he had mastered the techniques taught by this master, he retired to the north, to a place called Yamaguchi. It was an important cultural and commercial centre, presided over by a powerful family called Ouchi which was also in charge of Japan's commerce with China. Sesshu went to live in their family temple, but was soon

[1] I am indebted for much of this material to a lecture given by an American Professor in Tokyo at the time I was there.

requested by them to go to China on their behalf. This was the beginning of a new phase of tremendous importance for him.

He fulfilled his obligations to the Ouchi family on reaching the Chinese mainland, but his real object was to pursue further the Zen teaching and, with this in mind, he went to the famous Zen monastery on Mount T'ien-t'ung, near to the port of Nangpo where he had landed. He stayed many months there and was so highly thought of that he was given the seat of honour next to the abbot.

But he moved on northwards to Hangchow and Suchow until finally he reached Peking. As he went he made hundreds of tiny sketches; of landscapes and every kind of animal, of houses, pagodas and people. He went in search of Chinese masters who could teach him anything further about painting but he found no-one to rival those of the Sung and Yuan dynasties.

At the age of fifty, he returned to Japan, and, building his own studio at Yamaguchi, which he called the heaven-created painting pavilion, he began to put all he had learned into the masterpieces which are among the treasures of mankind.

There he painted daily until he died at the age of eighty-six, having subdued the fluctuations of his mind and made his heart like snow.

His painting was the result of life-long meditation, of his effort to live the meaning of his name, snow-boat, to become the One and overcome the many.

It reflects the all-embracing quality of his inner vision and his power to see Heaven in earth, and the Divine Essence in a leaf, the whole Universe or the most insignificant details of daily life.

> The wise man looks into space
> And does not regard the small as too little
> Or the great as too big
> For he knows that there is no limit to dimensions.[1]

It is this vision of Life, present in every brush-stroke, that strikes the sleeping soul like a thunderbolt and compels it to awake.

II

Angkor is myself. The path through the jungle leads to the temple of life.

As with the first meeting of the self with Self, all imaginative preparation vanishes in a moment of shock.

[1] Lao-Tze.

Those who go there enter a jungle that is light, high, beautiful; a tangle of green and gold. The sun shafting downwards through branches of giant fromager trees brightens their leaves, blanches their trunks, releasing the smell of bitter wood and fungus decaying in the subsoil dampness of last year's rainy season, and the scent of flowers clambering on vines towards the sky. Monkeys romp noisily through banyan and bamboo – but all rests upon silence.

Strewn over an area of roughly thirty square miles of this jungle are the ruins of a thousand buildings which from the ninth to the fourteenth centuries were built by a people called the Khmer. They lie on a battle-ground where forest wars with stone, where the slow insinuation of python-like roots has wreaked devastation. White tentacles cling limpet-close, pinioning as a falcon pinions prey, struggling to shatter the ancient harmony of grey stone and red earth. Their swifter rhythm of life has heaved and toppled cyclopean blocks, leaving them scattered, like mammoth bones after a cataclysm.

Some of these buildings, like the temples of Angkor Vat and the Bayon have been restored by the French Ecole de l'Extreme Orient. Some, like Prah Khan and Ta Prohm, are sinking deeper into gloom. Some glitter far from Angkor – like Bantei Srei. Others lie still un-discovered.

Everything not built of stone or brick has perished – the wooden houses, the tiled and painted roofs, the perfume and the precious stones. Only the temples remain and the roads flung like javelins across the land. Along these, first to conquer, then to defend, once marched the Khmer Kings – 'the dust of whose armies blotted out the sun'. They had ruled an Empire which at its height had numbered thirty million people and had stretched from the Bay of Bengal to the South China Sea, from the frontiers of the Celestial Empire to the Malay Peninsula. Where now there is the jungle, there had been the shimmering beauty of a city reflected in water, and, beyond, the green rice.

Who were the Khmer whose city was the priceless jewel of Asia?

In the first century and probably long before it, the banks of the three great rivers of South-East Asia, the Irawaddy, the Menam and the Mekong, were inhabited by a race that is now given the name of Mon-Khmer. Their origin is still obscure but they are thought to have come from western China.

To these communities which had already reached some degree of integration came people from the coastal areas of India. They, like the Phoenicians and the Arabs, were great traders. But they went one step further and settled here. Under the impact of the high civilization they brought with them, there developed the kingdoms of South-East

Asia. In Burma, there was the rich city of Pegu, and later, Pagan. To the south, there was Srivijaya with its capital in southern Sumatra. Its power and wealth made it Queen of the Seas and its influence and fame gave to the whole area the title of the Golden Chersonese.

Apart from these kingdoms, to the north there was always China, seeking tributaries and increased wealth. And to the west there was India and the immense expanse of the Kusana Empire whose frontiers touched the Gobi. From Kanishka's capital at Peshawar, scholars, monks and merchants moved eastwards along the arduous routes, bringing with them their learning, religion and trade.

The area that is now called Cambodia and Vietnam was in the centre of this plurality of power. The people that settled in the delta of the lower Mekong began, with the help of Indian engineering skill, to drain the marshes and build lake cities. By the fourth century they had amalgamated themselves into the kingdom of Funan – a name given to them by the Chinese. It became so powerful that a century later its only rival in South-East Asia was Srivijaya.

Most of what is known about Funan comes from the diaries of Chinese travellers. They describe its capital city as being full of canals. Boats coming from India or China could navigate right into its heart and there unload their wares. Merchants brought gold and jewels from India, porcelain, paper and fine silks from China. In exchange they received perfume, spices, the feathers of peacock and kingfisher, and rhinoceros horn.

Indian priests taught the people of Funan the Hindu religion and their sacred language, Sanscrit. They also taught them astronomy and mathematics. The rulers of Funan were said to be exiled Princes of India. They built their temples on high ground, and, like the Sailendras in Java, their title was 'King of the Mountain'.

But in the sixth century, either by terrible floods which wiped out the elaborate system of irrigation on which its existence depended and/or by its subjection to the Sailendras, Funan was virtually destroyed.

Meanwhile, further to the north, the kingdom of Chen-La had developed, until by 617 it was described by the Chinese as a land where thirty cities flourished, each boasting thousands of houses.

The following two centuries, which were the time of the apex of the Sailendra's power in Java, are obscure. But in 802, shortly after Charlemagne was crowned Holy Roman Emperor in Europe, a king called Jayavarman II, ruler of the Two Lands, Funan and Chen-La, asserted his independence from the Sailendra king, chose Angkor as the site of his capital and founded the first dynasty of the Khmer.

Angkor was a brilliant choice for a capital. It lay at the highest navigable point of the Mekong and close to the land route linking India with China. The Khmer were not slow to develop its immense potentialities.

People who visit Angkor today see only the jungle and are not told about the water. Yet at one time, Cambodia was covered with water right up to the foot of the mountains in the north-west. Only gradually was this reduced by the silt-depositing action of the great river. At the time of Funan, all that was left were the great lakes and marshes. The Khmer, profiting perhaps from the experience of the Funanese, took over their theories of irrigation and improved on them. They also inherited the intricate cosmological system associated with them that had come originally from India.

In the eleventh century, they built two immense reservoirs called barays and a network of canals which stretched far beyond the confines of the city. In the rainy season the barays were filled by the force of the swollen river rushing into them. Built as they were above the level of the plain, in the dry season water could be released through sluices into the canals and irrigate acre after acre of rice fields. To prevent the floods that had devastated Funan, the whole area was protected by earth dykes. From June to November, Angkor was an island in a great lake, but in all months a city of canals.

Irrigated in this way, the land yielded several crops of rice a year. This was more than enough to feed the entire population. The rest was bartered, for the Khmer, like the early Myceneans, had no currency. Their wealth depended on their rice and this upon their skill as engineers.

Temple building was simplified by this system. Each part of the city was connected with every other and with the outlying districts by canals. Stones could therefore be brought from the quarries right up to the site of the temple by water. This explains perhaps, the incredible fact that the temple of Angkor Vat was built in the short time of thirty-seven years.

Angkor Vat is exactly what legend says it is: the prototype on earth of the Palace of the King of Gods. It has God-like dimensions, being the largest temple still standing that so far we have discovered. Its design and execution seem beyond the scope of any man's talent. The symbolism of its structure was designed to lead man to God.

Unlike all the other temples at Angkor it faces west – the direction of death – and at sunset its grey stone is molten in the fire of the setting sun. The tremendous façade flashes golden in the waters of the moat. Five towers, symbols of the five peaks of the Holy Mountain, Sumeru, blaze beyond a blackening abyss of stone.

The moat encircles the quadrangle of the temple's outer walls for over four miles and is spanned on its western side by a causeway leading to the main entrance. From here, another causeway, far longer than the first, raised several feet above the ground and guarded by the fan-like cobras[1] that are the leitmotif of Angkor, leads to the mountain of chiselled stone that the Khmer called the Prasat. Immense and always distant, magnetic, it draws one towards it by a succession of passageways, galleries, terraces and steps. The nearer the approach, the more inaccessible it becomes. Repeatedly the goal is lost sight of, blocked by immovable stone. With ever-increasing impatience one speeds towards it – past myriad blurred faces of celestial dancers, swaying beneath the weight of marvellous headdresses; past walls and lintels where leaves and flowers interlace to form the gardens of Paradise and where visions experienced in a sculptor's heart have been projected onto stone. The sun filtering through columns illumines at intervals statues of the Bodhisattva sitting on the coils of his royal serpent-protector, Mucalinda, or a king triumphant upon his elephant with the ranks of his army tensed for the discipline of war. It softens the agony of animals transfixed in mid-flight by a thudding spear, and the sad, upturned faces of the vanquished. It restores animation to the exploits of the heroes of the Ramayana and to the cosmic feats of Vishnu.

The long wandering ends at last in one of the flights of steps leading to the Prasat. Thirty-eight steps, each so steep that anyone climbing them sees only the one in front and has to cling with prehensile fingers to avoid slipping, lead to the summit. Turning around, one looks back over the long way travelled as if at the vista of many lives; down steps, galleries, causeways, over earth and water to the green of the jungle, and sees the whole temple as a dark jewel in a setting of jade.

Standing there, questions rise in the mind. What is the peculiar quality that places this temple beyond the scope of description? As an architectural achievement, it can be seen in terms of measurements and proportions; as a feat of human labour, in terms of numbers, exploitation and tireless effort; as a work of art, an example of the limitless frontiers of man's capacity to devise and create; as an expression of Khmer wealth, in terms of the gold that once covered its towers and the revenues devoted to its building and maintenance; as an indication of the importance given to religion, in terms of the thousands of priests who once thronged its stone galleries.

But beyond all these, there is a quality that makes a person who has been there aware that he has with him permanently the memory of

[1] Symbol of the power of Consciousness, Kundalini.

92

this experience, and that its full meaning, though faintly apprehended, will only be understood aeons later.

Perhaps this quality springs from the fact that Angkor Vat is the description in stone of man's journey towards the Holy Mountain. It may be an expression of a king's pride and power but it is also one of man's purpose and destiny. When he has reached the inner room, the hidden chamber in his own being, symbolized by the sanctuary of the Prasat, he enters into communication with the Divine World and his journey is at last comprehensible.

This symbolism – to be found alike in Christian, Hindu, Buddhist and Muslim tradition – is what gives this temple vital significance.

Each place has its music and the chord of Angkor is majestic, hopeful, aspiring, leading to the dimension of achievement.

And because the inner vibration is so real, one stands listening for Angkor to take up again the rhythm of its life; listening for the hum of a million people at work, for the murmur of fifty thousand chanting monks and the swish of their robes on temple floors; for the tinkling jewellery of the dancers weaving magic in ritual patterns of movement to music; the trumpeting of elephants outside the city walls; the splashing of water as the court revels at midnight on the great lakes; the gay laughter of the palace women.

But there is only the silence.

It is one's companion in temples like black honeycombs whose labyrinthine passages seem only to lead deeper into gloom. The end is always ten yards distant, but the fugitive patch of daylight ever recedes beyond the stone images of the Buddha or Siva that are telescoped behind one another through numberless courtyards. The air is foetid with the smell of bats and animals that have slept there for centuries; the only sound one's sandal striking stone.

These temples are tortured by trees, dying of suffocation. But there are others whose sun-flamed pyramids gleam through the jungle. Flights of steps lead upward from one graded tier to another until they reach a wide terrace where in a towered sanctuary a lingam stands, or a statue smiles, recalling splendour.

The earliest of all temples at Angkor, the Bakheng, was built at the end of the ninth century to follow the contours of a natural hill. It rises steeply from the plain in a tremendous staircase. Once it had led to a platform crowded with four hundred small towers, arranged to portray the map of heaven, for the Khmer, like the Chinese and the Chaldeans, were skilled astronomers.

There is much that is mysterious about these temples. Why, for instance, do the sculptures of the Khmer kings and Gods bear an unmistakable Egyptian character? Why do their bas-reliefs remind one of Assyrian friezes on the walls of the palace of Senacherib, and equally of the Mayan sculpture of Yucatan?

Was there perhaps one parent civilization thousands of years before what we now call the 'Dawn of History' which gave these various descendants their tradition, rituals, beliefs?

All that can at present definitely be established is that the Khmer were influenced principally by India and China. Beyond that is ignorance.

Yet the two great temples of Angkor Vat and the Bayon, built respectively in the early and late twelfth century, are the unmistakable creation of a small group of individuals, perhaps even of one or two men. They may have studied the Hindu cosmology or the Chinese and Indian methods of temple building, but the result of their meditation is outstandingly and unmistakably Khmer.

There is a legend that the temple of Angkor Vat was copied from one that had existed centuries before on land which now lies beneath the sea between Java and Borneo. This was said to be the site of a great capital and the plans of the temple were so sacred that the knowledge of them was transmitted orally from generation to generation until it became possible to build another of that scale and dimension. Perhaps this explains why the first impression Angkor makes is one of ancientness, older even than Sumeria or Egypt. With astonishment one reads in the guide book that its great age of building corresponds with the Cathedral Age in Europe.

⋆   ⋆   ⋆   ⋆

Angkor is not one but several cities. Its kings, either through pride in their name or to resist the attacker and rebuild what he destroyed, built ever better and more magnificently.

In 1177 everything not built of stone or brick was destroyed by the invader's fire. Jayavarman VII returned from an exile he had imposed on himself and, at the age of fifty-five, began to set his kingdom in order. He undertook a programme of building fantastic at any period and which gave to the Khmer the title of master-architects of Asia. He surrounded his new city with walls fifteen feet high and over eight miles in perimeter. These he reinforced with earth-works on the inside and with a crocodile-filled moat on the outside. There were five entrances to the city, one for each of the cardinal directions and the fifth for his personal use. Five great causeways led to them across the moat, and on each one, forming colossal balustrades, crouched a double row of giants, Gods on one side, Demons on the other, holding in their arms sections of the sacred serpent.

The causeways with their guardians and the serpent – which in the East is a symbol of wisdom and power as well as evil[1] – represent the Rainbow Bridge that man has to cross on his way from Earth to Heaven. From the five gateways that symbolize the five elements of the soul[2] that are to be known and transcended, avenues led straight to the temple at the exact centre of the city. The man entering those gates who had any knowledge of Hindu cosmology knew that this temple was himself and that the broad avenues of his soul's long pilgrimage would lead him ultimately to the One Who awaited him in his innermost being.

Above each of the five gateways, Jayavarman set four great stone heads; two looking right and left; one frowning upon the outside world; the other gazing into the green wilderness that was once his city. Their diadems had shone golden in the sun. Standing beneath them, dazzled by the grandeur he saw before him, the traveller would have looked towards the centre of the city, at the strangest, most hallucinatory of all temples – the Bayon.

Today, however, the forest has devoured most of what gave the city coherent form. One comes suddenly upon the Bayon as upon a colony of gigantic grey ant-hills. It has not been restored to the same perfection as Angkor Vat and only as one climbs upwards through its dark passages and out onto the main terrace, can one grasp the magnitude of its design. Then it seems that the rest of the city was its precinct; the distant heads over the gateways, its guardians; and all within, its servant.

There, so close that one is almost stifled by the pressure of their gaze, are the brooding, secret, meditative faces of an infinity of Gods. They spring from the terrace as in Greek myth soldiers sprang from the dragon's teeth – fifty towers looming seventy feet above the ground, clustering about a central one that rises as high again above them. Each is sculpted on four sides with the same features as the Gods at the city gates. Their diadems curve into the petals of a lotus crown. Their eyes, washed by the rains of countless monsoons, seem both closed and open. Spread flat against the stone, their ears listen to catch the sound of the vision seen by the eye. Their mouths wear the archetype of smiles and express an inner peace and a harmony absolute. Whichever way one turns, there are the sharp angles of their profiles or the sunfullness of their faces. Now plunged in the shadows cast by their neighbours, now bone-white and dazzling, their interlocking gaze

[1] According to the context in which it is used.
[2] Earth, water, fire, air, ether.

95

forms such a magnetic field of power that the mind's only reaction is utter astonishment.

Jayavarman called his city Angkor Thom – Angkor the Great and great it must have seemed to anyone entering its gates.

Some say that these strange faces represent Jayavarman himself and that the temple is a monument to megalomania; others that they portray the Buddha or Siva or Brahma.

The Bayon is a Buddhist temple since Jayavarman is known to have been a devout Buddhist of the Mahayana school. The faces would, therefore, have a Buddhist connotation, representing both the Buddha and man as he is in the state of Illumination. This interpretation offers no contradiction to Hindu doctrine since the teaching of Hinduism and Buddhism is essentially the same.

The Khmer went through phases of both religions and sometimes the two existed side by side. Nothing in the cults of Siva or Vishnu denied the value of the Buddhist ritual. There were thousands of monks and priests in each large temple – many of whom no doubt observed merely the outward forms of ritual. There was also the mass of people who retained their far more ancient animistic beliefs. But they had no difficulty in grafting onto these the vast pantheon of the Hindu Gods or the Deities of Mahayana Buddhism. For them the vast temples they helped to build were an extra guarantee of their security. For a long time they were content to live in the most splendid city in Asia, content to gaze at the golden lotus that rested on the topmost tower of the Bayon and from it draw reassurance that all was well and that their God-king was protecting them.

But to Jayavarman and the priests who understood the inner meaning of these teachings, there was a greater responsibility. He interpreted the cult of God-king (Deva-Raja) in its highest sense. Where other kings of Angkor may have used it as a convenient means of reinforcing their power and may indeed have built temples to serve their own glory, Jayavarman did neither.

His rôle as king was to govern and guard an Empire and this he did superlatively. But one has the impression that his inner aim was to transmute what he was into something finer, to become a little less Earth and a little more Heaven. Knowing, according to what he had been taught, the ritual value of constructing such a temple as the Bayon, he carved upon its stone the wish that all beings plunged into the Ocean of Existence might be brought out of it by virtue of his work. Bringing back the jewels and flowers of his dreams, he spread them in the shape of this great symbol before those who were looking for tokens to take up the path in their evolution.

He and those who shared his indefatigable aspiration towards the Absolute took as their ideal the great sages of Vedic India and the Buddha. As one of the Khmer inscriptions says, 'they revered those who, having seen the agony of the world and been tormented by it as a Mother would be, worked to deliver it by attaching to the concept of Illumination the jewel of their thought'. 'If anger or some other passion arose in their hearts, they were rapidly dispelled by submission to their Science, as tame serpents vanish, hypnotized by the Enchanter.'[1]

They undertook the building of their stupendous temples as part of the same Science. All who helped to create them felt they were taking a step forward in their evolution, and that, since every action has its effect, they would reap the reward of their effort in coming nearer to Nirvana. The few who knew a little more of what is a mystery to most, learned, by meditation and prayer, to use the force of Blessing in their work, their speech, the trivial actions of their daily life. By concentrating in this way upon the aim of attaining their own Illumination and release from the cycle of rebirth, they knew that they were helping to raise the whole of humanity by one fraction of a note in the Great Scale of Evolution.

*   *   *   *

Why, one asks, if the rulers and priests of Angkor were devoted to this aim and its practical application in life, is the history of Angkor as full of blood and battles, terror and decay as any other Empire?

Perhaps it is because one man's vision can raise the level of a community's sense of purpose for a short while. But those who come after forget and the old pattern of a multiplicity of conflicting aims is re-established. Not only must there be continuity of leadership in this sense, but also a constant increment to the number of people who think and act single-mindedly. Only then can the pattern of the living death be broken.

The real disaster now as then is not the ever-present threat of physical destruction to civilization, but the refusal of mankind to invest its genius in the venture of the soul's destiny, instead of in the struggle for power; to aspire to the sun instead of continuing to divide the spoils of earth.

*   *   *   *

The Bayon was the last achievement of the Khmer in an architectural sense. But a hundred years later, Angkor still glowed with the brilliance of an emerald. Destruction had not cast more than its shadow. Festivals

[1] Quoted from *Angkor* by B. Ph. Groslier (Arthaud).

97

were frequent and on these days the dusty avenues of the city were cooled with water. Around the many temples flapped and floated thousands of silken banners. People left their homes and gathered along the King's Way, eagerly watching for the great procession.

A Chinese visitor described it as follows: '. . . First came the cavalry, and reaching above the clatter of horses' hooves, there arose the sound of many instruments. Then came battalions of women, marching in formation, wearing skirts of pleated brocade and hand-painted linen. Though it was broad daylight, they carried lighted candles. Then came chariots drawn by goats and horses, caparisoned with gold. And after them nobles and officials without number, mounted on slow-moving elephants and sheltered from the sun by red parasols. But these paled in comparison with the Queen and her suite, who were borne on palanquins and were of exquisite beauty in the radiance shed by a canopy of golden parasols. Then followed the King himself, wearing a crown encrusted with diamonds and standing upright on his elephant above a forest of white parasols. In his hand he held a magnificent sword and his elephant's tusks were sheathed in gold. . . .'

And the people, delighted, had returned to their wooden houses, which extended far beyond the city walls, and had spent the evening sitting on terraces open to the sky. They had seen their city illumined by a million lamps and 'on the elegant roofs had watched the peacocks dance and cry aloud'. They had passed the palaces of nobles whose houses' walls were fluted pillars or curtains of silk and brocade. And at dusk and dawn, they had gone to the deep pools to bathe and rested long in their moss-green shadows; men strong and dark-skinned who wound their hair into a top-knot; and women, fair and delicate-featured, who adorned their hair with jewels mounted on springs, or the flowers of jasmine and yling-ylang – whose presence was delight.

A hundred and fifty years later, by 1420, the golden lotus, the golden lions of Angkor had been plundered by the enemy. The Thais had wiped out a civilization as completely as the plague. Those of the people who remained alive fled in horror from the place and established a new capital at Pnom Penh. Angkor became the haunt of the spirits of the dead, cut off too swiftly from a life they loved. Of the fantastic treasure nothing remained. All that was left were the temples, infected by an unnatural silence, inhabited only by animals and creeping roots.

They lay there, with the breath of their life cut short, long abandoned by love, decaying in magnificence, until in 1870 a man stumbling through the jungle in pursuit of a legend came suddenly upon them and restored their treasure of symbolism to the world.

III

Bali reflects the higher state where earth is not seen as earth, but as Heaven.

Two thousand miles of rich land, cultivated meticulously and with ceremony; once part of the great land belt linking Asia with Australia, a place where known and unknown civilizations have met and mingled – this is Bali.

It is an island whose people look not to the sea which they fear but to the mountains, the abode of their Gods. Their terraced earth, so marvellous to the eyes of the traveller, is only one of their seven worlds and the first of their heavens.

Legend says that they came from a great city in the west of the island which even now exists, invisible.

Their life, like Siva, has many faces, each one evoking with its smile a different aspect of beauty.

Their guiding principle is a mystical compass, a microcosm of themselves, whose north is always towards their Holy Mountain and whose south is always the sea. They call it the Rose of the Winds.

★　　★　　★　　★

In Djakarta there is a museum which should be the pride of Asia. Upstairs, in a room lined with red velvet, is gathered a golden treasure comparable to those of Carolingian or Renaissance Europe, to Mycenae or Byzantium. Whoever goes there before he visits Bali will ask himself: 'What is Bali that its people could work such perfection with their hands?'

In this room are displayed the regalia, the weapons, the jewellery of the Balinese, all in gold, all studded with sapphires, rubies, rose diamonds and emeralds; of exquisite workmanship and in a profusion that seems incredible.

From this alone, Bali would inspire curiosity; and secondly wonder; and thirdly, understanding of why, to the Balinese, there is Bali and there is the rest of the world.

Henri Rousseau, although he never went beyond the Jardin des Plantes in Paris for his leaves and animals, has captured in his paintings the very essence of Bali; its greenness, its clarity; its mysterious forest. It has, not a frightening forest, but a lush, light-reflecting, singing one, where the sun imparts brilliance to the thousand-threaded tapestry of trees. Each leaf is distinct, claiming recognition of its individual presence, its precise texture and shape. Every leaf, branch, tree and flower seems to move with a rhythm suddenly apparent because of the moment of mind-silence created by amazement. In breathing there is no loss; only an intake of wonder and an outbreathing of delight. The eye follows the leap of smooth trunks into the sky and the heart leaps with it. The eye penetrates the labyrinth of banyan and rests there in darkness.

There is the scent of dusk when earth exudes the warm fragrance of day. There is the frangipani petal and scarlet hibiscus trembled by the slight breeze; woodsmoke curling upwards from fire; water rushing brownly beneath bridges.

There are men and women like the golden figures on ancient friezes, wide-shouldered, narrow-torsoed, clothed in the colours of leaves and flowers, naked above the waist. Their feet walk firmly upon earth and their hands seem made to convey meaning by gesture or to hold great vases delicately. They move as if they are notes of a symphony – in harmony with each other, conscious of immortality. They walk through their forest to the world they come from, the perfumed heavens of the Ones they worship, calmly and with grace.

In the blue-blackness of earliest morning, there are the sounds of people stirring, preparing rice for the day's meals. Here and there a shuttle clicks, weaving splendour.

And on the beaches, where the sand is still cold from night, all waits for the roar of the sun's rebirth. In the great silence, fishermen lift their nets high against the shimmering gold and the drops of water fall back rainbowed into the sea. Women work among the rocks at the water's edge, gathering crabs and coral into baskets which they swing without effort onto their heads, moving in slow procession along the shore.

The pathway of the sun widens swiftly until all the sea takes fire and the women are silhouettes. Long after they have gone, the men continue to fish far out on the coral reef, or in boats with prows carved like elephants' trunks, painted with eyes to see in the dark, and triangular sails unfurled to catch the wind.

And in the evening there is dancing, and, at all times, music.

★   ★   ★   ★

Bali today gives little indication of its turbulent past. Yet since the arrival two thousand years B.C. of a people thought to have come from southern China, there have been few intervals of peace. The Balinese, who seem so conscious of their difference, have absorbed Chinese, Polynesian, Hindu, Malayan, Arab and European elements, all of which have been superimposed upon a distinctive Megalithic culture.

It was said at one time that 'when three thousand rainy seasons have passed, the eastern islands will again be reunited and the power of the white man will end.' Perhaps the prophecy is beginning to come true.

Three things have emerged from a violent history: a concept of the community that has been integrated by centuries of successful practice; a way of life that rests upon fundamental religious beliefs and rituals many thousands of years old; and a mastery of music, dancing and art that is as extraordinary as it is peculiarly Balinese.

None of these may endure under the impact of 'enlightened Indonesian policy' but they existed still when I was there four years ago.

The unit of organization has always been the village and the whole island is really a federation of economically and politically independent villages. Each is governed by a council consisting of all the married men and an elected and unsalaried headman. For convenience, it is divided into sections, called bandjars. The bandjar is a co-operative society, with a communal bank, its own temple, kitchen, orchestra, dance costumes and public meeting place. If it is rich enough to build more than two temples, it becomes a village in its own right.

In theory, all the land in Bali belongs to the Ancestral Gods who delegate their authority to the council and lease the land to the community. In fact, the council controls the distribution of land to the individual members of the community and has the right to take it away if anyone is considered lacking in civic responsibility. The produce of the land belongs in the first place to the Gods, and only secondly to the community.

A system of reciprocal economic assistance, whereby all members of the village are provided with food and shelter, has up to the present time made possible the great amount of leisure devoted to the constant feasts and festivals that are the duty as well as the joy of every Balinese, and the very essence of his life.

It is not surprising that the worst punishment for a man who has injured the community is to be exiled from his village. This means that he is automatically expelled from every village on the island for a crime against a part is a crime against the whole. His existence is on a level with the animals who roam the desert in the west of the island.

The entire wheel of life in Bali is minutely regulated by magic and every village and house is laid out according to the formula contained in the sacred compass, the Rose of the Winds.

Through the centre of the village runs a spacious, tree-shaded avenue, one end pointing to the Holy Mountain, Agung, and the other to the sea. Another crosses it at right angles and the place where they meet is the sacred heart of the village. Here cluster the huge banyan tree, the temple and the Prince's palace, the market, the communal kitchen, the orchestra platform and the shed for cockfights. Here the men gather in council and the women in trade.

The whole village is surrounded by a high mud wall, punctuated at intervals by narrow entrances that lead into the separate family compounds. Each one of these is an organic unit with its own kitchen, shrine and living quarters. The houses are built up a yard above the ground, inaccessible to dogs, chickens and floods. Some are open, with removable bamboo walls. They have roofs of thick, smooth grass, supported by a framework of pliant bamboo poles that converge towards the apex like the rays of the sun.

From dawn onwards, the centre of the village is alive with noise and bustle. Women come walking down the narrow dusty roads into the shady avenues, moving with an easy, graceful stride and carrying on their heads loads weighing as much as fifty pounds; sheaves of rice, coconuts, terra-cotta water pots, offerings of fruit and vegetables or lacy pig's fat for the temple – all balanced upon a slender-necked stand which rests upon a scarf wound round and round the head to form a cushiony turban and one of the most flattering headdresses ever invented.

There are never any men in the market. Women control the entire transaction, sitting or standing behind their wares, shouting the prices, bargaining, smiling. The place is like a superb coat of many colours. Each woman wears a different kain – a slender cocoon encasing her from waist to ankle, patterned with flowers or leaves or butterflies against a soft and faded background of green, brown, magenta, mauve or lilac. Their skin gleams from effort in the sun and their dark hair is coiled in a hundred different ways, intertwined with scarves or flowers.

The old are not ugly because they retain the slim bodies and fine bones of the young. Their smiles embrace all living things.

The heat brings out the odour of dried fish, spices, flowers and vegetables. Pigs squeal, voices hum and colours dance in the light filtered through banyan and bamboo.

Along the sides of the two great avenues are many food stalls. With the rice that is the basis of their diet, the Balinese eat pieces of highly spiced meat, cooked deliciously in aromatic leaves; or delicate sweets of fruit steamed in banana leaf or cooked in coconut cream and cinnamon. On special occasions they eat dragon-flies in coconut oil. At all times they have as much fruit as they want; mangoes and mangosteens, melons, papaya and breadfruit. They never use plates and are generally silent when eating. It is the special privilege of the men to prepare the food in the village kitchen for the many feasts, and turtle meat, dipped in coconut cream and roasted, is their chef-d'oeuvre.

Around the stalls, chatting happily and stroking their prize roosters, while taking bets on them for the next fight, squat the men, while the women transact business. Children play in and out of the high door-ways that lead to the family compounds, utterly content. They have a rare dignity and self-possession from the time they begin to walk. Always in the company of older people but never scolded or dismissed as nuisances, they learn to take part in the most sophisticated con-versations, to look after themselves competently and to enjoy the rich variety of their life.

Through the village moves a perpetual procession of pink or brown buffalo, ridden by boys who are content to spend in this way the hours required to get their beasts to and from the water. They ride from the gloom and comparative coolness into the dazzling brightness of the rice fields, protected from the heat by huge straw hats. Flight upon flight of terraces, cultivated with infinite care to the last inch, rise like a great staircase to the sun; squares of green side by side with squares of clear water which mirror the blue of the sky.

Like Persephone, the Balinese Goddess of fertility, Dewi Sri spends half the year below the earth with Vishnu, Lord of the underworld. But in Bali, she has much work to do because there are two rich crops of rice a year.

The Balinese worship the sun, earth, mountains and sea as sources of fertility, and the rice is nursed to ripeness by constant ceremonies and offerings. Once a year, a pilgrimage is made to the sacred sources of water in the mountains and some is brought back to the rice fields to ensure a good crop. An elaborate and admirable system of irrigation brings the water down from the mountains and allows every separate field to be flooded or drained when required. Shrines with tiny thatched roofs stand isolated in the greenness and here, once a month, gather the men responsible for the welfare of the crop.

This one example is an indication of how closely interwoven with Balinese life are the threads of magic. Forty-two days after he is born, a child takes part in the first of an endless series of ceremonies, and is given his secret name by the priest. Soon, it is as familiar to him as the rice he eats that his world is peopled by three kinds of Beings – Gods, Humans and Demons – and that each has his appropriate dwelling: Gods in the mountains, Demons near the sea, and humans in the between-world.

He learns that there are seven heavens and that earth is the lowest of these. The second is the middle sky – the great blue dome we see in the daytime. After that is the cloud sky where the God of Love has His Kingdom; then the dark blue sky of the sun and moon; the perfumed sky of the flowers and falling stars; the heaven of the Ancestors; and, last of all, the heaven of the Great Gods Who watch over All.

He respects and worships his ancestors, who include the heroes of Hindu mythology, like Rama, and his own beloved King, Erlangga, who lived in the eleventh century. They are the intermediaries between him and the Great Gods, Whom he calls Bataras.

Siva is the greatest of these, but Siva is the Name given to the Cause and Essence of all things, Who, centuries ago and even now in many parts of the island, is called Tintiya. Everything in the seven heavens is a manifestation of Him. Under various names, He is found at the source of rivers, in every tree and flower, at the heights of the mountains and the depths of the sea. He exists as the Spirit of man in every part of the human body, but is concentrated in the head and the heart.

Bali experienced four great religious influences. In the seventh century there was Mahayana Buddhism when the island was under the power of the Javanese Sailendra dynasty. In the ninth century, there was orthodox Sivaism, followed by Tantric Buddhism in the eleventh century and Hinduism of the Javanese kingdom of Majapahit in the fourteenth.

Elements from all of these were grafted onto the far more ancient and deeply rooted system of ancestor and spirit worship. Today it is hard to tell what belongs to which religion, so closely integrated have they all become.

Between the people and this pantheon of Gods and Demons stand the Brahman priests who alone have the power to interpret Their Will. They alone know the secret mantras and ceremonies inherited from the Brahman and Tantric priests of India and Tibet. They are the only people on the island to speak Sanscrit and, therefore, to be able to read the scriptures containing these formulas. They have the right to intone the sacred syllables of the Rose of the Winds, whose unified sound is Ong (Om). They know the mantras which can summon the Gods of the cardinal directions. They can invoke an ancestral spirit or induce a trance state. Most important of all, they are able to tell men how to maintain the correct balance between positive and negative forces which is the essential condition of a harmonious existence on earth.

They are accordingly revered and many Balinese wish to reach the spiritual level in this life where, in the next, they may be reborn as a Brahman priest.

Balinese dancer (author)

Borobodur (author)

An aspiring Brahman priest has first to learn Kawi, which is the Balinese language of poetry. He is taught that the capital sins are anger, greed, hypocrisy, envy, ill-temper and morbidness, apart from theft and murder. He learns to cultivate an attitude of detachment to but not withdrawal from life. When he has mastered this much, he learns Sanscrit and studies the Vedas. Finally, when his teacher considers that he is ready, he is initiated by an elaborate ceremony. His body is washed as if it were a corpse. He passes through a symbolical death and is reborn into his new level of being, less fettered by ignorance, more harmoniously in contact with the Divine Principle in himself.

Belief in reincarnation is the keystone of this elaborate structure of ancestor-worship, placation of witches and demons, and offerings to the Gods. This Life is part of a long cycle of rebirths, but the way in which it is lived is of vital importance since it affects the state in which a man is to be born in his next existence and accelerates or slows down the pace of his journey towards Enlightenment and release from samsara.

> Karma accumulates through lack of knowledge;
> Karma is the cause of rebirth;
> Through knowledge it comes about that no Karma is effected;
> Through absence of Karma there is no rebirth.

The Balinese know, or are told by the priests, that to the Great Gods, nothing is of value save the growth of the soul and the gradual deliverance from the illusions of earth; that to Them it is a time of rejoicing when a test can be given and a soul raised a step nearer to Them. Therefore, they are told to keep their goal ever before them and to realize that the purpose of their life on earth is to learn how to reflect the Divine Will. They are told not to mourn in their exile but to make of their life a joyful ritual and to await patiently the time of the Coming-forth. They believe that the steadfast man can climb to the stars.

For these reasons, their religion is not an abstract set of theories but a way of life. As far as possible, every act is directed so that it comes close to the point of balance between positive and negative forces, just as the great Lord Siva rests at the heart of the Rose of the Winds.

The village, the houses, the eating of food and an infinite number of what to us are unimportant, everyday things are minutely regulated by the formulas associated with the magical compass and interpreted for the people by the priests.

If a man is in harmony with the hidden forces round him, he is encouraging a quality in himself that the Balinese call 'sakti' which means the capacity to reflect God. Some people, like the priests, are born with a greater proportion of sakti than others who have to work to develop its growth. Disharmony or the upsetting of the balance in a human being or a community by a bad mental state or action results in the loss of sakti and causes a condition called sebel. When a man or a village or the entire island falls into this state, he is greatly weakened, defenceless, open to the attacks of Demons. The balance can only be restored by elaborate rituals, purification rites and offerings to the Ancestors and Protective Deities.

This is the general background to the endless ceremonies and feast days, when no offering is accepted at the temple unless it is well made and beautiful; to the ritual dances and shadow-plays; the exquisite costumes; the cremation pyres where months of preparation costing thousands of pounds vanish in the flaming moment of the soul's release from the body; to the sculpture and painting of a whole people, gay, witty, Cretan in their sophistication to whom art, like dancing, is communication between Earth and Heaven.

In all their work – and each has many skills – there is no sense of competition. No work is ever signed. The climate with its humidity and heavy rain shortens the life of any work. Temples, paintings, sculpture, costumes decay and crumble and are at once renewed, always in traditional style but often with modern elements incorporated. Nothing is ever lost and nothing really dies.

There is no aspect of their activity that does not portrary Bali as it is to them – an island pervaded by presences; an island of sheer marvel.

But of all their accomplishments, dancing is the most vital and astonishing expression of their essence. They attribute a divine origin to music and dancing, believing that the first instruments were invented by the Supreme Teacher of mankind.

The cremation ceremony is a time for laughter and rejoicing for it celebrates the liberation of the soul rather than the death of the body. In contrast to it, the ceremony of the dance is an experience of wonder and awe and those who watch it are silent.

The time for dancing is the evening or late afternoon, when men and women have bathed in the deep pools, cool in the dusk. Then, refreshed, the women with jasmine and frangipani threaded through their black hair and the men with a scarlet hibiscus behind the ear, gather near the great banyan or before the temple.

Night falls.

The light from a lantern illumines the intent faces of a group of little girls who are being made up by their relations. They have started their training at four years old. At eight they are at the height of their powers, and at thirteen too old to dance the most perfect of Balinese dances, the Legong. At first they are taught by the older girls in the village who were formerly dancers, and later by a renowned teacher. Constant repetition makes the movements of arms, hands, legs, feet and head automatic. Their bodies, made supple by endless practice, are fluid and sensitive to each vibration of the music. They learn to carry without fault the elaborate costumes of the Beings they embody.

Their make-up consists of a thick dusting of rice powder which transforms their faces into white masks. Black eyebrows, lipstick and a series of white dots on the forehead and at the corners of the eyes are added.

When this has been completed, the costumes are brought out; a long sarong, scarlet and gold, trailing on the ground; over this a piece of white cloth wound like a tight bandage from breast to hip; a long scarf, of different colour and design from the sarong, wound to follow the intersections of the binding; a straight apron, hanging from breast to knee. Then are added the jewelled armlets and anklets, a necklace of beaten gold, gold cylinders which fit into dilated ear-lobes and finally the headdress which all this time has been prepared. It is the symbol of the sahasrara padma or thousand-petalled lotus of Enlightenment. More sumptuous than any crown, heavy with flowers of hammered gold and fragrant with the petals of frangipani which are set in one by one to form a halo, it shimmers and trembles as it is placed on the head.

Already absorbed in their rôle, serious and unsmiling, the little girls enter the temple to be blessed by the priest before the performance. Touching each one on her face, head, tongue and limbs with a flower, he inscribes with it the magic syllables that invoke the power of the Spirit to animate the body.

Like the temples all over Asia, those of Bali symbolize the Cosmic Mountain, Sumeru, the Inner Spirit. Here they have three courts, representing the three levels of man's being; body, soul and Spirit.

While the little girls are inside the temple, the musicians begin to gather round the steps, dressed in emerald green kains and red turbans flecked with gold. They settle themselves and their instruments around the edges of a large square of rattan which serves as a carpet for the dancers.

The entire set of instruments is called a gamelan and is the property of the whole community. Over seven thousand of them exist on the island, each one of which is tuned slightly differently from every other. Each village has its musical club whose members practise continually until a new variation is ready for a public performance or until they are called upon to play at a temple festival. This explains the sounds to be heard at any time of day all over the island. There are twenty-five to thirty members in each gamelan who can play every instrument. The two most outstanding musicians are chosen to be the drummers, since they lead the group. The gamelan consists of bells, cymbals and gongs, through whose resonance the flute weaves melody and the drums rhythm. No music is ever written down.

A flight of steps leads down from the temple to the square of rattan and on either side of these stand the two white parasols that throughout South-East Asia are the symbol of royalty. Tall flambeaux cast their light down upon the musicians, defining the flowers and vines carved upon their instruments, and the pure gold leaf; and up onto the rosy walls of the temple, drawing all into the circle of their radiance and barring entrance to the night which listens outside.

If it is the time of the full moon, there may be the dance of Rangda. The story is one of the most told in Bali.[1] Erlangga, the hero-King of the eleventh century, had a mother called Rangda, who because of her witch practices, was banished to the jungle. In revenge, she used every means in her power to destroy her son's kingdom. Desperate, Erlangga at last sent for the great sage Bharada and begged him for his help. Bharada sent his handsome assistant into the jungle in search of the witch's beautiful daughter, whom hitherto the nobles of the island had been too frightened to marry. He, however, protected by Bharada, succeeded in marrying her and persuaded her to borrow the magic book her mother used to cast her spells. This was copied and returned without its loss being noticed. The book was a sacred one, which when read backwards as the witch had been doing, reversed the powerful white magic and transformed it into evil. Then ensued a great duel between Bharada and Rangda, ending in the death of the witch by one of the sage's mantras.

But the Balinese, anxious to propitiate, do not allow the story to end in her death, hoping thus to gain her goodwill and parry her destructive spells.

The music of this dance is, if anything, more haunting and beautiful than that accompanying any other.

Rangda's attendants appear first, moving as if under a deathly spell, with their hair hanging over their faces and threaded with jasmine flowers so that they look as if they had been pulled, half-drowned, from water. They wear saffron sarongs and their torsos are swathed with gold leaf.[2] Their nails are elongated into gold claws.

For a long while they dance. Then, with a shuddering howl, the

[1] The symbolical meaning of it may no longer be taught but the intuitive understanding of its significance has not yet died.
[2] This is not a fixed costume, only the one I saw.

witch herself appears, freezing the audience with horror by confronting them with a hideous embodiment of evil. So powerful is the violence of her possession that her vehicle has been known to go insane.

This is only one dance of many; every one fascinating; some moving; some terrifying. They lead one into ages far beyond recorded history and our meagre knowledge of ten thousand years.

Of all of them, however, the Legong is the most beautiful and the most famous.

Before it is danced, there is always a rippling thrill of anticipation in the crowd.

Two little girls, swaying to the music like celestial flowers, descend the temple steps, holding with raised arms the dishes of offering to the Gods. There is a moment of pause and the Legong begins.

Three little girls sit waiting; two of them dressed in royal costume, the third as their attendant. She now appears from the temple steps, moving as if in trance, drawn by the music to the centre of the square of rattan. Suddenly the music pierces her with a violent rhythm, sending the flowers of her headdress swirling about her, galvanizing her limbs into a whirlwind of movement. The music becomes more gentle; she stoops to pick up two fans and is joined by the other two. Together they weave a pattern so intricate, so exquisitely beautiful that it seems to the audience that these are no children dancing but Beings of Fire and Light – Messengers of the Gods.

The first dancer withdraws, leaving the other two to dance the story of King Lasem. The foregoing was but an introduction. They dance the love of the King for the Princess Rangkesari, and her rejection of him. They tell how he abducted her, how, when she wouldn't submit, he threatened to kill her father in battle. Their fluttering fans become the raconteurs: delicate as the wings of a dragonfly; swift as the king-fisher plunging after prey. They speak of grief and despair, anger and lust. They are the deadly keriss, poised to strike death.

The battle is set, the tension of the music unbearable, when suddenly there is a new theme and the third dancer enters again, this time with great golden wings bound to her arms. She is the blackbird, destined to thwart the evil intent of the King. With leaps accompanied by the crash of cymbals she joins the battle, flapping her wings so swiftly that all the air is gold. Thrillingly the music vibrates as she obstructs the King, obscuring his vision until at last, defeated, he falls dead. The story is told. The dancers, without a sign of tiredness, again become little girls.

There is an interval and the Kebyar is danced. This time, the dancer is a boy, chosen as are all the children for the emotional intensity they are able to convey together with their musical sense and their skill. He never rises from the ground. From beginning to end, like a swaying cobra, he hypnotizes the audience and the musicians by the extraordinary expression of his eyes and the movements of his hands. Taut, tense, fantastically alive, his torso darts from side to side; the jasmine flowers on the small turban vibrate; the golden hibiscus trembles over one ear.

★   ★   ★   ★

These dancers are not in trance. They are absolutely detached from any personal emotional participation in what they are doing, yet intense concentration is required to convey to the audience the emotions of the story. Although each physical movement is automatic through long practice, their performance is always individual. Their dancing has a magnetism that is found nowhere else in Asia, perhaps because when a Balinese dances, he is immersed in the Immortal, communicating with That in himself that is the source of life and form and movement. Entering into himself, surrendering himself to That, he enters into all people and expresses in his dancing the fact that all are of One Nature, children of the same Father, with the same needs and like destiny.

★   ★   ★   ★

As for the music of Bali, he who has once heard it, will never forget it.

At first there is a waiting, a silence so heavy that it can be weighed and measured.

Then, as if it comes from the breathless forest, there is a sound, the fragile tinkle of bells.

It grows in volume until the heart aches with an Orpheus-like longing and the temple seems to tremble with its vibration. At the beginning, it is water-filtered, muffled, as if rising through the sea from some lost continent. It ripples the way the Greeks carved waves on stone.

Then it becomes the language of Rima, the warbling notes drawn from the harmony of Nature. It has the sharpness of new rice piercing damp earth. It flickers like the fiery worlds where flames do not burn but transform.

The ear adjusts itself slowly and slowly the being attunes itself to an utterly new experience. And then the mouth curves into the smile of eastern and archaic Greek sculpture – the involuntary smile of ecstasy. Every sense strains to listen, to the tinkling of bells in a minor key, like the first thrilling touch of a lover's hand; to the notes of a flute beckoning through seven heavens; to drums like the rhythm of interstellar shuttles, weaving the garment of a greater destiny; to the crash of the gong that unifies all worlds and brings the mountains to the sea.

Something stirs and wakes and remembers a resolution made long ago to rest like a drop of water upon the petal of a lotus. The insistent repetition of one theme brings one to the threshold of revelation and a forgotten sentence from the Orphic Mysteries rises into the mind:

'I am a child of earth and Starry Heaven, but my race is of Heaven alone. O give me quickly to drink of the cold water that comes from the lake of memory.'

And although there is no immediate answer to this appeal, the theme of the music is perfectly clear at this moment. Its communication, hundreds, maybe thousands of years old, originating in the unknown temples of unknown civilizations, is the story of the struggle to awake and the journey towards Self-consciousness. It is the thread of Ariadne, leading through the labyrinth into the Presence of the One within.

IV

Borobodur! Borobodur! A word like a trumpet-call from a temple in Java that is always a sanctuary.

★ ★ ★ ★

Java is a land seen in a dream, rising from the sea in long green slopes that curve upwards into the cones of active volcanoes, and nowhere is the unreal quality of the landscape more apparent than in the country around the ancient capital of Jogdjakarta.

It lies nine hours' train journey south-east from the depressing modern capital of Indonesia. The sordidness affecting the cities of Asia has not yet touched it. There is still dignity, beauty and a measured tempo of life. It is one of the few places where there is relief from the intolerable tension in other parts of the island; from the atmosphere of violence that hangs like a pall of evil over the population that is not fortunate enough to be isolated in the jungles.

A little after dawn on a steamy, tropical morning, the road from Jogdjakarta to Borobodur is like a ribbon of white silk, blackened here and there by people wheeling their produce to the city. Far away in the left distance is a jagged line of peaks, just piercing the mist that shrouds the whole plain. To the right is Merapi, most fearful and dreaded of volcanoes, destined one day to erupt simultaneously with a tremendous earthquake that will split the island in two. At this hour only its central portion can be seen. The rest is hidden by mist and cloud. It is like a mountain in a Chinese painting, its power increased by invisibility.

Borobodur could only have been built in that one place in the centre of the plain, on a mound surrounded by jungle.

From the air it looks like a huge grey wedding-cake. From the ground, it is a confusing mass of stone, rising in tiers and dotted with hundreds of small statues seated in niches. Above them on the upper terraces is a forest of bell-shaped stupas with an immense one crowning the top.

It was built some time in the eighth century during the rule of the great Sailendra dynasty, to contain, like Sanci in India, the ashes of the Buddha. The pilgrim should enter at the East Gate and move round the successive terraces to the left, so that the ashes of the Buddha are always on his right side.

Borobodur was built at a period when Mahayana Buddhism was at the height of its influence. It is a mass of seated stone figures. What do they represent? Who are they? Why are there so many? Sooner or later one has to answer the question: What is Mahayana Buddhism? Historically it is the form of Buddhism that took root in Tibet and China and that infiltrated from here into the kingdoms of South-East Asia. At first it seems to consist of a vast number of unidentifiable Gods, each one with a name difficult to pronounce, whose particular attributes are hard to recognize in the sculpted figures of Mahayana temples or shrines. Associated with their worship are sacred mantras (sounds) mudras (gestures) and mandalas (written symbols) which to the unsympathetic eye appear to be just plain magic or, more contemptuously, superstition.

It is a pity that the interest of so many people should be killed by their contact with the sharp frost of this kind of criticism, and that their attempt to understand Buddhism in any of its forms should be arrested by the words 'nihilism', 'pessimism', 'pantheism' and 'superstition'.

The entire stupa of Borobodur is a documentation of the evolution of a man from the person he is to the Being he may become.

Whether the sculptures are seen as descriptive of the life of the Buddha or of the life of the person looking at them, it is the same. The path of Gautama like the path of Christ is the path of anyone who wishes to follow it.

The outer wall and lowest section of the stupa is sculpted with scenes from the daily life of man. The first four square terraces have narrow galleries like an Egyptian tomb but they are open to the sun. A series of hundreds of panels relates on one side the experiences of the Buddha in his former incarnations and in his future one as Maitreya;

and on the other side his life as Gautama, son of the King of Kapilavastu.

The three upper terraces are circular and have no sculpted panels. Instead seventy-two seated, meditating figures preside, each almost hidden by a bell-like cover perforated by square or diamond-shaped holes.

The highest terrace is crowned by a solid stone stupa which is said to have contained a statue of the Buddha turning the Wheel of the Law. Beneath it was a crypt – symbol of the sanctuary in the heart.

In this journey from Earth to Heaven, man is not without help. As he walks the path around the terraces, gazing at what he is and can become, he is surrounded by a multitude of presences who at every stage offer their guidance and assistance if only he can become aware of them. They are not remote Gods whom he must placate and worship as personifications of abstract principles. They are aspects of himself. They symbolize the inner states of being; of highest wisdom, knowledge and harmony that he will one day discover and experience. Other men before him have done this. Their achievement is expressed in the forms of the great Dhyani-Buddhas of Mahayana tradition. If he meditates upon them; loves them as the Guardians of the Way; tries to understand the meaning of the qualities associated with them and to reflect them in his own life, he will embody them, for in fact they are himself. When he visualizes them in meditation, he is giving form to the latent forces within him that will help him to reach Enlightenment. By recognizing them, he gives them power to act. Until this recognition takes place, they are his enemy, strewing his path with trials and suffering until he is forced to acknowledge their presence. They are cruel and pitiless until, by his own act, they become wise and loving. So it is that Yama, the Lord of the Dead or of this world where man lies in his death-like trance, becomes Avalokitesvara, the Compassionate One, when the trance is broken by desire for Life. So it is also that the Buddha Gautama, who may at first be worshipped as a God, in time becomes the Friend because it is realized that He has experienced the same titanic struggle and His attainment is eternally present to encourage and inspire.

Then there is only one desire: to become like Him.

This is the meaning of Borobodur and the countless figures of the Dhyani-Buddhas crowding its terraces. They say to the pilgrim:

He who wants to avoid the hundredfold pain of existence,
Who wants to still the sufferings of sentient beings,
Who wants to enjoy the hundredfold happiness,
Such a one must never abandon the Thought of
Enlightenment.[1]

[1] From the *Path towards Enlightenment* by Santideva.

And when he has understood what it means to become a Bodhisattva, he may speak the vow that they have taken before him.

'I take upon myself the burden of all suffering. I am determined to endure it. I do not turn back. I do not flee, neither do I tremble. I fear not, I yield not, neither do I hesitate – and why? Because the deliverance of all beings is my vow.

'I am working for the establishment of the incomparable realm of knowledge among all beings. I am not only concerned with my own salvation. All these beings must be rescued by me from the ocean of Samsara by the vessel of perfect knowledge.'[1]

To help him fulfil this vow, he has only to call upon the Dhyani-Buddhas for guidance.

At Borobodur, facing east with his hands performing the mudra (gesture) of touching and blessing the earth is the Dhyani-Buddha Aksobhya who embodies the Wisdom of the Great Mirror. If the pilgrim will meditate upon what in him should reflect and What should be reflected, he will attain to the Wisdom of the Great Mirror. If he will purify his mind from attachments to all lesser aims, he will allow it to reflect the True, the Infinite, the Universal Consciousness.

Facing south, performing the gesture of giving, is the Dhyani-Buddha Ratnasambhava who embodies the Wisdom of Equality. If the wanderer will strive to understand that all men are equal because the Divine Nature is present in all, he will overcome the illusion of a separate existence and realize his identity with the One in all, and the all in One.

Turned to the west the Dhyani-Buddha Amitabha makes the gesture of meditation. His is the wisdom of the Infinite Light and the Unfolding Vision. If the seeker after Light will steadfastly pursue his Aim, he will find that, like a flower opening to the sun, his intellectual faculties and his sense perceptions will expand to include the faculties of intuition and direct perception of truth.

Facing the north is the Dhyani-Buddha Amoghasiddhi who embodies the All-accomplishing Wisdom, performing the gesture of fearlessness. He is that power in awakening man which encourages him to proceed from one discovery to another; which will not let him rest until the final one is experienced and the searcher is one with the Object of his search. Through his constant activity, the knowledge gained by insight is slowly translated into action until the stage of the Deed of Liberation is reached. The Karma-bound activity of the unenlightened man becomes the creativity of contemplation incarnated in

[1] From the Vajradhvaja Sutra, both quoted by the Lama Govinda in *Foundations of Tibetan Mysticism* (Rider).

114

deeds. Amoghasiddhi is therefore Lord of the Great Transformation.

To accomplish the transformation, there must be no fear. Of all barriers, this is perhaps the most difficult to overcome. When trembling on the edge of the abyss of self, the seeker of the Philosopher's Stone should call to mind Amoghasiddhi's gesture of fearlessness which is the quality of all Bodhisattvas. When recoiling from suffering, he can say: 'Everything that happens to me, whether joy or suffering, I will accept fearlessly because it leads to the Light.'

The topmost stupa conceals or concealed the Dhyani-Buddha Vairocana, the Illuminator, the Radiating One who turns the Wheel of the Law, and is the embodiment of the Wisdom of the Universal Law. 'The one who is perfect in his faith, his concentration and his knowledge cannot fail to attain liberation.'[1] The person who walks along the galleries of Borobodur knows that if he can but attune himself to the movement of the Great Wheel, it will surely bring him to Enlightenment. He must learn how to set his foot on the path. He may say with the words of the Tibetan Book of the Dead which was written for him, the living-dead:

O that now, when the Bardo of life is dawning upon me
After having given up indolence, since there is
no time to waste in life –
May I undistractedly enter the paths of listening,
reflecting and meditating
So that . . . having attained human embodiment,
No time may be squandered through useless distractions.

According to another interpretation which, in slightly different words, reaches the same conclusion, the sculpted terraces of Borobodur tell the story of Sudhana.[2] After going through the repeated experiences of daily life until he wants to know the purpose of existence, Sudhana hears from the Buddha Manjusri about the deeds of Gautama and declares his desire for Illumination. Manjusri is the wielder of the sword of discriminating knowledge that severs the knots of ignorance (an aspect of Amitabha).[3] Sudhana, having listened to this voice in himself, begins to look for a living teacher, since Gautama is no longer alive, and one by one visits thirty, each of whom gives him a thread of the Traditional Teaching. After many years and lives of search and effort, he comes into the presence of the Buddha Maitreya (He who is

[1] The Lama Govinda, *Foundations of Tibetan Mysticism* (Rider) to whom I am indebted for much of this interpretation.

[2] As recounted by Heinrich Zimmer in *Art of Indian Asia* (Pantheon) and taken from a Buddhist text called the Gandavyuha.

[3] He corresponds to the Archangel Michael of the Christian tradition.

to come). Maitreya sends him back to Manjusri who in turn sends him to Samantabhadra, who represents the furthest stage of development. Under the tuition of the highest part of himself and after long practice of meditation, Sudhana becomes an initiate and experiences Enlightenment. He enters the Diamond realm of Vajrasattva – 'He whose essence is the Adamantine Bolt'. He has ascended into Heaven and brought down Heaven to earth; He is able to think, speak and act for the benefit of all that lives. He has achieved the synthesis of wisdom and love, knowledge and compassion, light and life. He can wield Vajrasattva's adamantine bolt of Pure Consciousness and is the embodiment of Avalokitesvara or Active Compassion, combined with Wisdom. Beyond this there is no further going.

Mahayana Buddhism is not magic in the common sense of the word but it is Magic is the sense of the Science of self-transmutation.

The witnesses to the truth of this symbolism are the Ones Who have achieved Illumination, Whose lives are the expression of At-Onement with the Divine Essence. They are not one or two but many; a few known; the rest unknown. But the Way They walked is unmistakable to anyone who can see the signs and Their attainment has raised the level of all mankind.

The Dhyani-Buddhas of Mahayana tradition are no different from the Angels of Christian and Hebrew tradition or from the Greek or Norse Gods.

It may be that there is a great hierarchy of Beings Who watch over the world, our planetary system, the Cosmos.

But the way to know Them is not to ponder the problem endlessly with the intellectual part of the mind, to state whether They or God exist or don't exist. Until the furthest limit of the mind's development is reached, how can I know what is or is not? The vow to be taken is: 'Whatever be the highest perfection of the human mind, may I realize it for the benefit of all that lives.' When I have become that highest perfection, I will know.

To do this I have first to listen to the voice of intuitive feeling that leads me to accept the teaching of the Tradition. Later I may come to understand it intellectually. It will make sense. If I persevere, intuition and intellectual conviction together may be transformed into spiritual certainty by direct experience of Reality.

So I say with the words of Hermes Trismegistus: 'Ye Powers that are within me, hymn the One and All; sing with my Will, Powers all that are within me.'[1]

*   *   *   *

[1] G. R. S. Mead: *Thrice Greatest Hermes; the Secret Sermon on the Mount* (Watkins).

Because of the confusion of life, the pulling this way and that by a multitude of emotions, duties, desires, fears, in the midst of which the One is forgotten, there is need for places of sanctuary where, for a few moments, all noise subsides and there is silence.

At the very top of Borobodur, after climbing the terraces and watching the sun transform the cold grey-black stone into the golden warmth of Sicilian temples, there is sanctuary. Even the breeze ruffling the palm-fronded plain is inaudible.

Two of the stupas covering the Dhyani-Buddhas have been removed to reveal the statues and these convey absolutely the brooding impression of peace that is the quality of Borobodur.

For twelve centuries they have sat unmoved by tumult, in the same way as all the Buddhas have sat through the night of Their Awakening, unmoved by Mara's efforts to shake Their resolution. Withdrawn, compassionate, gazing beyond the horizons of the world, they are that part of man that is not subject to growth or decay, but is eternally living in his heart, eternally waiting to be recognized and loved. For this reason they remind of purpose. They inspire hope. They convince that truth is accessible and help available and that the Holy Mountain on which they sit is to be climbed within man's being, here and now, in life.

With one powerful voice they cry:
'Incomparable are the WAKE.'

V

India speaks through poetry and sculpture and painting. The outer forms are dead but the inner Spirit is awake, ready to be reborn. The courtyards of the temples are dusty but on the walls are the Gods and the truth is there to be seen. There is Vishnu ever waiting to be born from the cosmic ocean; Durga, ever riding her lion and killing the buffalo-demon; Ganapati, ever watching over the crossroads of choice; Brahma, the ineffable, ever waiting to be recognized; and above all Siva, dancing the cosmic dance that creates, preserves and destroys and brings all fragments to unity. The figures are so majestic, so beautiful; the symbolism so clear that it is in these places that I would bow my head in gratitude to the One Who has brought me to them. For I see now that part of me is Durga[1] and part the Buffalo-demon and part the lion which carries her to victory; one in me is Ganapati helping me

[1] Durga is an aspect of the Great Goddess who is known variously as Kali, Parvati, Hecate, Hera, Maya, the Virgin Mother, etc.

to choose the path of liberation instead of death. Brahma is My Self; the One to be born from the Cosmic Ocean of my being is Vishnu; the One who dances the dance of transfiguration in my heart Siva, and all these are aspects of the One and All. When I gaze at them, I look at the One I am. There is no pride here; only amazement that this is so; that the work of transformation; the destruction, the creation, the preservation of the universe that I am is the work of the Great Dancer and that the scene of His Dance is myself.[1]

Indian temples are not relics of the past. Their sculptures are not obscene; nor do they simply express the physical union of man and woman. In the clearest possible way they use this symbolism to awake in the heart of the beholder the knowledge that there can be no peace in man or on earth until soul and Spirit are united in the cosmic embrace. Sexual desire is a symbol of desire for eternal life, for truth and for God. Its union is the symbol of atonement of soul and Spirit, the Mother and the Father, of the outer world of Form and the inner world of Being.

And if a Christian standing before these symbols should wonder what there is in his own tradition that can compare with this, there is the question once asked: 'When shall the kingdom come?' And the answer: 'When the two shall be one and the without as the within and the male with the female neither male nor female.'[2]

This symbolism is diffused all over India. Wherever there is a temple or a shrine, there are men and women, Gods and Goddesses embracing; wherever there is the worship of Siva, there is Siva's Lingam – the pillar of stone resting on the circular base – the Yoni. Some may see it as worship of sex; others as worship of Siva; others as worship of Being in its Receptacle, Form, and will relate it to themselves and understand the nature of desire which, according to their use of it can hold them to Earth or bring them to Heaven.

*   *   *   *

The same ideas are reflected in miniature painting.

The technical brilliance of Indian miniature painting owes a great deal to the influence of Persia, and through Persia, China and Byzantium whose paintings and illuminated manuscripts found their way to the Persian courts in Herat, Tabriz and Bokhara. At the time of the Moghul invasion of India in the early sixteenth century, some

[1] For a complete analysis of what the figure of Siva Nataraja – Siva as the Cosmic Dancer – means, see Ananda Coomaraswamy's *The Dance of Siva* (Asia Publishing House).   [2] From the Gnostic Gospels.

of the artists of Babur's court went with him to his new capital at Delhi.

His grandson Akbar was the true founder of Moghul painting for he drew from all parts of India those who wished to share in the Imperial patronage. Two Indian painters, Daswanth and Basawan, became as famous as the Persian Bihzad.

The paintings of Akbar's and his sons' court are largely concerned with the events of court-life, but another style rapidly evolved which combined Moghul technique with the ancient Indian legends like the Ramayana or the life of Siva or Krishna.

The artists of Rajputana, the Deccan and, later, the states in the Punjab hills – Guler, Kangra, Jammu, Basohli, and Garhwal – learned from the Moghuls their manner of portraiture and the various techniques for applying colour and at the same time preserved what existed of their own decaying tradition and gave it new life. They were more interested in portraying the everyday life of the people and the Hindu legends than the life at court.

It is in their paintings that one can find the mystical reflected in the everyday, Heaven on earth.

The court of Akbar, who was the contemporary of Queen Elizabeth I, became the focus of a renaissance of the Hindu Legends of the Ramayana, possibly under the influence of a great poet called Tulsi Das. Music, dancing, painting – all became vehicles for the expression of different parts of the legends. Eventually the Ragas,[1] the paintings or the dances became so concise that it was possible for an artist, hearing a melody, to paint the scene associated with it or for a dancer to 'dance' the picture.

Painting, music, dance, poetry – all are ways of coming closer to Reality. Akbar himself said that he thought a painter 'had a quite peculiar means of recognizing God' and perhaps for this reason, since his life was a search for the Absolute, he learned to paint himself. 'Let a man with firmness separate the spirit – the Inner One – from his own body, as a fibre from a painter's brush.' A painter in trying to discover himself through his painting then or now is doing no more than this. Often and often this verse from the Upanishads must have been meditated upon.

As the apprentice learned the art of which paper to use for what picture – the fine variety from Samarkand or Cathay and the coarser one from Isfahan or Kashmir – and how to extract colours from stone or rinse them from earth he may – if he were mystically inclined – have compared this work with that of self-discovery. He may have recognized

___
[1] The melodic forms of Indian music.

the parallel between this work and that of gathering the material of many lives, re-membering himself, refining himself, preparing for the Great Experience. As, completely prepared, he put his first brush stroke upon paper and saw before him its dazzling effect, he may have realized that the brush, like the body, is the instrument. The work it does depends upon the quality of the artist's being, and the extent of his contact with God.

In the eighteenth century, a little over a hundred years after Akbar's death, many artists, frightened by the ever-increasing violence of Akbar's grandson Aurangzeb and the dissolution of the Moghul Empire, took refuge in the Rajput courts of the hill-states north of Delhi. There they produced the exquisite works known under the name of Pahari Miniatures.

Many of them illustrate the infinite aspects of the love story of Radha and Krishna. Looking at them, I enter a world of love – not only love between man and woman which is shown as it can be – but love pervading every facet of life. For the first time perhaps, I see why it is so important to carry love into as many activities as possible. Every gesture, every expression of love is a vital strand in the rope linking Earth to Heaven.

In the presentation of woman as she would like to be, beautiful and beloved against a background of leisure and passionate desire to be united with her love, there is the symbolism of the greater longing and the greater union. The love of Radha for Krishna, her waiting for him through nights of storm and days of preparation for his coming, is the reflection of man's longing for union with his Other, True Self. In these paintings the two levels of life, the outer and the inner, the visible and the invisible, are linked by the understanding that one is the symbolic reflection of the other and by the love that is the way to their embrace and union.

Here in the symbolism of sex, the pointed cypress trees, the still pools, the piled-up storm clouds and the flashes of lightning which pervade every painting with an atmosphere of tension and urgency, is also the higher interpretation to which all these symbols belong. There is no divorce here between the apparent and the real. Far from it. Sex rightly interpreted, rightly used, is a method of knowing the truth of which it is the symbol. Sex transfigured by the love and tenderness that Radha and Krishna have for each other can bring man closer to the experience of Being and for some it can be a gateway to realization of how the whole of life can become transfigured in the same way.

This is a different representation of sex from the one we know today. The distortion of the teaching about control of sex into the attitude that

Awaiting the Lover: Nurpur *c.* 1790 (Victoria and Albert Museum)

Tun-Huang (Photograph by courtesy of Mrs N. J. Chakravarti)

it is something evil and shameful is a further lamentable proof of the degeneration of religion.

East and West sex is considered to be a necessary evil and control of it is interpreted to mean total or almost total abstinence. One who could prove that he was beyond this temptation has in the past been considered a saint. In India this control is called brahmacharya, in the West, celibacy. In both places, it has at times beome an end in itself.

From this distortion which has existed for hundreds of years, have resulted the sexual neuroses that plague both civilizations. One of its results is the attitude common to both, that woman is 'the temptress', which has been responsible for far more evil in the form of her persecution and suffering than her 'temptations' have ever been.

Brahmacharya applies primarily to control of the lower mind. If there is control of the passions of greed, hatred, lust, jealousy and pride, there will automatically be control of sex because the misuse of sex springs directly from these passions. The man or woman who is jealous, who desires to possess, dominate or control the other, who has contempt for the act of sex and performs it furtively, guiltily, or cruelly, or who is preoccupied with thinking about it is misusing it. He or she has no idea of what brahmacharya is.

When the passions have been recognized, admitted and controlled, the whole conception of what sex is and how one should use it is transformed.

There is no merit in continence at the physical level. A person who tries to abstain, who thinks that because he doesn't perform the act he has control of the sex-impulse, who imagines that he is more 'spiritual' than the person who does, who is called a saint by the world because of this apparent 'mastery' of sex, is deluding himself as well as the world. He can be as much a victim of his lower mind and his phantasies as the man who declares he is free of all 'inhibitions'.

True brahmacharya is manifested at an advanced stage of the Path when control of sex exists because the passions of the lower mind have been overcome. It is then not an effort, not something which a man struggles to maintain or even that he is conscious of having. It may not necessarily mean abstinence. It is the natural outcome of his having reached a higher level of consciousness and a deeper awareness of the unity of all things.

★　　★　　★　　★

Woman is shown in these paintings as she longs to be loved; not possessed by a stranger with whom she cannot communicate, but united with one who takes as much as she can give and gives as much in return as she needs, with whom there can be expansion into ever new planes of awareness because there is mutual purpose and perfect understanding.

Then all that destroys is left behind because there is no room for it; the 'rights', the hurt pride, the resentment, the urge to hold, smother, annihilate the other.

Here there is the small gesture of affection and the holding close in darkness so that there is the reassurance of another sharing the experience of night. Here love assuages loneliness and fear is banished. There is laughter all day long over little things.

In the night of the wrong relationships when men and women are out of communication with each other, estranged from love, what can assuage loneliness? Who, in the bitterness of her own disappointment, her fury that the other has not given her what she demanded, can hear his plea for help or the cry of his despair? Who can transform a life of antagonism into one of love?

The answer is in the symbolism of these paintings. If there is love of the Self, all the rest will come right.

In the fragrant silence of a summer night a woman waits, certain that her lover will come.

So the soul waits and longs for the Beloved.

So earth waits for the joy of union with Heaven.

Part Seven

I

IN KASHMIR, THERE IS TIME TO LISTEN TO THE VOICE
that penetrates the confusion of thought.

It is ringed by great powers, eager to exploit or defend the fair,
strategically vital land.

So is the soul ringed by the powers of fear, greed, anger, jealousy
and pride; subtle, clever and hard to overcome.

If I were a statesman and did not know myself, would I serve
humanity, or these powers? If I have no peace in myself, how will the
voice of wisdom be heard amid the roaring of so many lions? If I serve
the lesser gods, how will I reflect the guidance of the Counsellor, the
love of the Prince of Peace?

Until I know myself how can I diagnose what is wrong with the
world and realize that what happens there is the reflection of what
happens in me, and that the wars and fears and exhibitions of anger
and greed are the outer manifestations of the disordered inner world of
the mind?

Am I to remain like the world where every part is the enemy of every
other because there is no allegiance to what is beyond all of them, yet
contains them all?

If I do not surrender to love, how will I overcome these powers that
hold the world and myself in thrall? How will I forget self interest and
serve the Self?

I see that nationalism is like the lower mind. If there is no growth
beyond it, it breeds fragmentation and destruction. It sows the same
seeds in a larger field; pride, resentment of rivals, desire for revenge,
greed, egoism. It, like the lower mind, struggles to resist surrender to
a higher purpose. It tears the world to pieces just as the fallen mind and
emotions lacerate the inner world of man. How many disasters, national
and individual, are the result of this cause? How often is God blamed
for them, or Fate?

If nationalism and the lower self are not transcended, if there is no
thrust of growth towards the Whole, there must inevitably be dis-
integration, atrophy and death.

In man, it is the second death.

In the world it is annihilation by war.

If I would help the world, I must know myself. I must separate my watching self from my participating self and identify myself with the first so that I can rule the other. Then gradually, the lower will serve the higher.

If unity is to become the law of earth, it must first become the law of my being.

In face of the threat of this dual destruction; knowing that if I do not work to be One, I can lose my soul, how could I choose otherwise than for Life?

This is very clear to me now, in Kashmir, but will it be clear when I come down from the mountains and return to the separate allegiances of my life? Will I be able to recognize those powers that lead to death and transform them into those that lead to life? Will they control me in the work that I do, whether I am a statesman, a scientist, a writer, or simply a wife? Or will they become servants instead of masters?

★   ★   ★   ★

Kashmir is like a painting I have seen.[1]

In a landscape blanched by moon radiance, lion and gypsy meet. There is no violence or terror. One watches; one sleeps. Such a meeting is not yet for us who drive away our lions. We do not lie in cosmic silence upon the desert of the world, guarded by kings.

At night, earth and sky are blue. In the lakes shine the snow-crested ones. Lotus drowse. On his shikara a man sits listening – holding his paddle above the water – to a woman who sings on the faraway shore.

It is possible to hear the song.

In the day among a crowd of shuffling people through the town of brown, dilapidated houses, a woman rides by in a cart. She is unveiled, beautiful. Amid the buying and selling who sees?

By a roaring stream, a boy prepares tea over a fire. Because it is dusk, I draw closer. He looks up and smiles.

Have I no rose to give him?

To him I say: 'Let me remember your smile like the lightning flash! I stand in awe of your beauty. Now I desire to lift my soul towards you and the great peaks. Teach me to love, that I may no longer hear the footsteps of the self; only the Sound beyond the little words, beyond the little words.

'Then one day I may return your smile as I drink the hot cinnamon tea you have prepared to warm me after the day's ending.'

[1] 'The Sleeping Gypsy' by Henri Rousseau.

II

Sometimes a parallel can be drawn between the inner world and the outer. Sometimes, one can see the world as a reflection of oneself.

I did not reach China. I call it Tafghach,[1] the Marvellous because it is the symbol of You and of myself. You are still beyond. But I know Who You are. I feel Your Presence.

I, like China, am struggling to go beyond what has kept me from You for so long; the old gods, the heavy rituals, the habits of thinking that suffocate the Spirit. I am in the twilight realm, neither wholly asleep nor yet awake, knowing what has to be accomplished and wondering when it will ever be done. I, like China, have the choice of continuing to act from my lower nature or of learning to act from my higher one. I can turn from You or move towards You. I am beginning to see the Power that You are, the Wisdom that You are, the Love that you are. How could I choose to follow the downward path?

You Who live forever because you were never young say to me: 'The approach to China is by river-roads and many caves, made marvellous by endeavour.

'In the Thousand-Buddha Caves of Tun-Huang a horse leaps through an orange sky and his rider's robe flickers like fire.

'Great Beings preside.

'The sands of Gobi conceal Shamballa, secret heart of the world.

'How shall you come there?

'O by much further wandering.

'Like the veins of the body are the avenues of approach to the Cave of Being; many streams flowing into one and that into the Heart and its recesses of splendour, where Fire is.'

I know that Your Voice which I can hear now and then when I clear away the sands of thought is the only guide out of the labyrinth.

'Strive to know yourself as That which is immortal.

'Surrender yourself to me,' You say. 'I am closer to you than breathing. Love Me and you will come to Me. The way lies upwards to complete at-one-ment with the One Who Breathes.'

I know that, step by step, You will teach me how to surrender and become Yourself.

I speak to You and say: 'I would be saved.'

You answer: 'And I would save.'

'I would be loosed.'

'And I would loose.'

'I would be born.'

[1] The name once given China by the Altaic tribes of Central Asia.

'And I would bring to birth.'
' I would eat.'
'And I would be eaten.'
'I would hear.'
'And I would be heard.'
'I would be at-oned.'
'And I would at-one.'
And again You say:

> 'I am a lamp to you who behold Me.
> I am a mirror to you who perceive Me.
> I am a door to you who knock at Me.
> I am a way to you, a wayfarer.
> You have Me for a couch; rest then upon Me.'[1]

Your Voice has led me through all the experiences of many lives, teaching me what had to be learned, showing me what could be seen, bringing me across the desert to the foot of the Holy Mountain.

III

I come there[2] after sunset when silence wanders over marble and grass, water and black cypress. As I pause in the entrance, looking as if from earth towards a distant planet, it seems to fill all space. Between us is a garden where a corridor of water reflects a fire-white star. It seems suddenly revealed, like the whirlwind answers that come years after prayer has begun.

I go closer, and removing my shoes, climb the stairs and come onto the warm white stones of the great terrace that encircles the tomb that is a temple. At the back, beneath a marble balustrade, the Jumna river flows. Beyond it, diminished by distance, is the Agra fort, where Shah Jehan spent seven years looking towards his wife's tomb and mourning the murder of Prince Dara, the son he loved.

I walk and walk, knowing the contact of skin with stone, of silk with marble, of the softness of my hand with the unyielding flowers of lapis lazuli inlaid in the walls or with one of the ninety-nine names of God calling to His world.

How, I wonder, can I integrate this moment in my memory so that no filament should be lost of the conviction that while I am here, I am partaking of all beauty, all endeavour, all achievement.

[1] From the Gnostic 'Acts of John' in G. R. S. Mead, *Fragments of a Faith Forgotten* (Watkins).   [2] The Taj Mahal.

Oh if I could, with the leap of the lion, accelerate the rhythm of my being; enter new dimensions of awareness where thought is no longer a reflex, but, tempered to precision, would flash like the sword of an angel.

Oh if the tomb could become the temple and Love descend intact through the seven heavens.

I sit by the river and wonder when earth and water and fire and air will be ready to receive the Sun. When will the four become five, and the five seven, and the two one? When will the outer be as the inner and the lower as the higher and the male with the female neither male nor female?

I pray to You Who wait behind the Far Walls.

I have no refuge other than Your Threshold.

Hear my prayer of longing. Help me to finish what I have begun, to bring to completion what I have undertaken, to fulfil the vow made before the beginning and after the end. I hold the thin white ribbon of light that binds me to You, knowing that it passes over all mountains to where You are waiting. I feel it threatened by the storms of despair that assail me. When will this work be finished and I come into the harbour, all journeying done?

You have put into my hands jewels gathered from the four corners of the earth. Help me to make of them a treasure.

Let me listen to what is said in the quiet places of the mist-filled mountains; let me sit under the spray of the waterfall and ride over the stone bridge that leads from here to there; let me rest among forests of bamboo and hear their rustling as the river flows by – deep flowing water which carries me to You. Somewhere a dragon thunders through the palaces of storm and I wait and watch and wait and am not.

Have I not waited since the beginning of my pilgrimage and wandered upwards to find the home of the heart in the hidden grotto? Have I not many times looked out over miracles of nature, the soft hills of the south and trees? And spent lifetimes learning how to make one perfect gesture of compassion, one stroke of the brush on silk that is the lightning flash, and wandered from temple to temple, kneeling before all the altars of the world?

I wait for the opening of the Way, for the power of Fire that will precipitate me through the Great Wall and into Your Presence.

And You say: 'Do not despair over your lack of achievement. It needs only a few years, days or hours of complete realization and service to make worthwhile the arduous way back to the heavenly spheres.

'Do not mind the seeds of the past but look up at the stars and wait for the vision that will entrance your sight.

'It is not easy to achieve the liberation of the Universal, the re-demption of the individual, yet it will be achieved and Unity become the law of earth!'

I warm myself with Your love and continue my walk through the night.

IV

In Crete there is the labyrinth built by Daedalus for King Minos. During the war the Germans used it as a storing place for arms and ammunition.

In the Cathedral of Chartres there is another labyrinth, described in stone on the floor of the nave. Most of the year it is hidden by chairs and few people notice it.

God is hidden in man, and the Tradition that could reveal Him is hidden also; in myths and fairy-tales, in scripture and in poetry, in alchemical treatises and astrology. Myths and fairy-tales are read by children and forgotten as they grow up. The twelve labours of Hercules, the story of Prometheus, the myth of Creation, the Iliad and the Odyssey, the tale of Snow White and the Seven Dwarfs are considered to be 'campfire stories' created for entertainment alone. The heroes fighting before seven-gated Thebes are of no interest to those who are not classical scholars or children. The Zodiac is no more than the path of the sun through the twelve constellations. Astrology has become character-analysis and prediction of future events. Tarot cards are for fortune telling. Holy Mountains and Gods are the inventions of primitive man. Plato's allegory of the cave has nothing to say to twentieth-century man. The Book of Revelation is incomprehensible – the work of a mystic. Joan of Arc's 'voices' were the hallucinatory results of her being riddled with tuberculosis. The Sleeping Beauty and Aladdin's Lamp are wonderful bed-time stories for children but are of no interest to adults.

The list is endless and the loss of the Tradition tragic. Man wanders in the labyrinth and is not even aware of it. He stands upon the stone floor of Chartres and does not see what is beneath his feet, perhaps because he is too busy looking up towards the vaulted roof. All around him is beauty and mystery and truth, but what is closest to him he does not see. He is blind to what could explain himself to himself. He searches for it all over the world, in a thousand different ways while it waits under his very nose for his recognition. The answer is simple but the search for it is not.

He goes East to find it and then returns to recognize it everywhere in the West. It may be covered with chairs, distorted, abandoned, the treasure of children under the age of ten and of mystics, but it is there.

Whoever looks for it with his whole heart will find it, and finding it will learn how to use it, and using it will solve the mystery of himself and discover the Way to God.

I repeat now what I said at the beginning of this book but now it is an affirmation.

There is One in me Who discards experience after experience, search after search, life after life until at last we meet face to face.

I have come from Unity into the separateness of existence, yet there is a way back to Unity through discarding of self and finding of Self.

I cannot experience the Resurrection before I have discarded the dead leaves, the outworn garments, the old wineskin of self.

While I do not know this I impede the Return. I am fallen, exiled, asleep. I lie as dead upon the streets of Egypt.

I will rise, awake and perform the Twelve Labours of Hercules.

This is an age of extraordinary darkness and extraordinary revelation. If I lie asleep, I am a prisoner of darkness. If I can awake, and learn how to restore the stolen fire to heaven I may experience the revelation.

I will awake from the first death so that I will not know the second.

I will understand the mystery of earth and water and fire and air.

I will follow the pathway of the Sun through the twelve houses of my being and become the Solar Hero.

There is One in me Who is my guide. It is He Who lives forever because He was never young. I hasten to meet Him but He is always with me. He is all the Heroes who show me the Way. He is the Seven Great Archangels Who are the messengers between Earth and Heaven.[1] He is the Celestial Hierarchies. He is my Self.

I listen to His Voice and try to understand the meaning of His words. I hear It in what comes to me as life, in what I read as the poetry, myths and revelations of all civilizations and all times; in what I see, touch, hear, speak and breathe. It tells me that all that I perceive with my five senses is Himself. It tells me how to awake my inner senses and to look beyond the changing forms of what is called the world to What is Eternal and Unchanging, to see all as the manifestation of the One.

---

[1] The Great Seven are Michael, Gabriel, Jehudiel, Raphael, Uriel, Barachiel and Sealtiel. They correspond in earlier traditions to the Sun, the Moon and the planets Jupiter, Mercury, Mars, Venus and Saturn, and to the Greek and Roman gods. They preside over the seven days of Genesis, or the seven stages of the spiritual path. They are the 'powers' in man which lead him to God. The Celestial Hierarchies and the Hosts of Heaven are also within man. When at last there is in him 'a multitude of the Heavenly Host praising God' then can take place the Divine rebirth and the Resurrection of the Seventh Day.

The Voice was once inaudible. I hear it faintly now. It tells me that I am Theseus and It is Ariadne's thread and the labyrinth is myself. Part of me is Perseus and part Medusa and one will have to slay the other. Gabriel's trumpet will announce the Divine Birth of the Son in my heart and will sound again when the Day of Resurrection has come. Michael hands me his Sword and says to me: 'Take it. I have brought it down from the Higher Heaven and kept it pure through my breath of Fire. It is yours if you see it. It is yours if you learn how to handle it.' And I know that the true use of the Sword which cuts the bonds of ignorance is the surrender of self to the service of the One, and that my work is to transform myself into the jewelled scabbard. The seven spheres and four elements are the levels and divisions of my being and the ladder up which I climb to Heaven. When the Sun arises in me the light of the stars will vanish and I will be free of their power. I seek the Grail, the Pearl of Great Price, the Treasure, and I am told to look for them in the Cave of my heart. When I have found them, the Mystic Marriage will take place. I and my Father are One. Samsara and Nirvana are One. Heaven and Earth are One and everything is God.

Drawing of the Labyrinth at Chartres
(by courtesy of Editions Houvet)

THE HYMN OF THE SOUL[1]

When I was a little child
And dwelling in my kingdom, in my Father's house,
And in the wealth and the glories
Of my nurturers had my pleasure,
From the East,[2] our home,
My parents, having equipped me, sent me forth.
And of the wealth of our treasury
They had tied up for me a load.
Large it was, yet light,
So that I might bear it unaided –
Gold of Beth-Ellaye
And silver of Gazzak the great,
And rubies of India,
And agate from the land of Kushan,
And they girded me with adamant
Which can crush iron.
And they took off from me the bright robe,
Which in their love they had wrought for me,
And my purple toga,
Which was measured and woven to my stature.
And they made compact with me,
And wrote it in my heart that it should not be forgotten:
'If thou goest down into Egypt.
And bringest the one pearl,
Which is in the midst of the sea
Hard by the loud-breathing serpent,
Then shalt thou put on thy bright robe
And thy toga, which is laid over it,
And with thy Brother, our next in rank,
Thou shalt be heir in our kingdom.'
I quitted the East and went down,
There being with me two messengers,
For the way was dangerous and difficult,
And I was young to tread it.
I passed the borders of Maishan,
The meeting place of the merchants of the East,
And I reached the land of Babel,
And I entered the walls of Sarbug,
I went down into Egypt,
And my companions parted from me.
I betook me straight to the serpent,
Hard by his dwelling I abode,
Waiting till he could slumber and sleep,

---

[1] By Bardesanes, a gnostic who lived in Edessa A.D. 155-233. Taken from the apocryphal 'Acts of Thomas' and quoted by G. R. S. Mead, *Fragments of a Faith Forgotten* (Watkins).
[2] The Spiritual Kingdom.

And I could take my pearl from him.
And when I was single and alone,
A stranger to those with whom I dwelt,
One of my race, a free-born man,
From among the Easterners, I beheld there –
A Youth fair and well-favoured.

★   ★   ★
★   ★   ★   ★

... and he came and attached himself to me.
And I made him my intimate,
A comrade with whom I shared my merchandise.
I warned him against the Egyptians
And against consorting with the unclean;
And I put on a garb like theirs,
Lest they should insult me because I had come from afar,
To take away the pearl,
And lest they should arouse the serpent against me.
But in some way or other
They perceived that I was not their countryman;
So they dealt with me treacherously.
Moreover they gave me their food to eat.
I forgot that I was a son of kings,
And I served their king;
And I forgot the pearl,
For which my parents had sent me,
And by reason of the burden of their ...
I lay in a deep sleep.
But all those things that befell me,
My parents perceived and were grieved for me;
And a proclamation was made in our kingdom,
That all should speed to our gate,
Kings and Princes of Parthia
And all the nobles of the East.
So they wove a plan on my behalf,
That I might not be left in Egypt,
And they wrote to me a letter,
And every noble signed his name thereto:
'From thy Father, the King of kings,
And thy Mother, the Mistress of the East,
And from thy Brother, our next in rank,
To thee our son, who art in Egypt, greeting!
Up and arise from thy sleep,
And listen to the words of our letter!
Call to mind that thou art a son of kings!
See the slavery – whom thou servest!
Remember the pearl
For which thou didst speed to Egypt!
Think of thy bright robe,

134

And remember thy glorious toga,
Which thou shalt put on as thine adornment,
When thy name hath been read out in the list of the valiant,
And with thy Brother, our next in rank,
Thou shalt be king in our kingdom.'
And my letter was a letter
Which the King sealed with his right hand,
To keep it from the wicked ones, the children of Babel,
And from the savage demons of Sarbug.
It flew in the likeness of an eagle,
The king of all birds;
It flew and alighted beside me,
And became all speech.
At its voice and the sound of its rustling,
I started and arose from my sleep.
I took it up and kissed it,
And loosed its seal, and read;
And according to what was traced on my heart
Were the words of my letter written.
I remembered that I was a son of kings,
And my free soul longed for its natural state.
I remembered the pearl,
For which I had been sent to Egypt,
And I began to charm him,
The terrible loud-breathing serpent.
I hushed him to sleep and lulled him to slumber;
For my Father's name I named over him,
And the name of our next in rank,
And of my Mother, the Queen of the East;
And I snatched away the pearl,
And turned to go back to my Father's house.
And their filthy and unclean garb
I stripped off, and left it in their country,
And I took my way straight to come
To the light of our home, the East.
And my letter, my awakener,
I found before me on the road,
And as with its voice it had awakened me,
So too with its light it was leading me

.   .   .   .

Shone before me with its form,
And with its voice and its guidance,
It also encouraged me to speed.

★   ★   ★   ★

And with his love was drawing me on.
I went forth, passed by . . .
I left Babel on my left hand,
And reached Maishan the great,

The haven of the merchants,
That sitteth on the shore of the sea.

★   ★   ★   ★

And my bright robe, which I had stripped off,
And the toga wherein it was wrapped,
From the heights of Hyrcania
My parents sent thither,
By the hand of their treasurers,
Who in their faithfulness could be trusted therewith.
And because I remembered not its fashion –
For in my childhood I had left it in my Father's house -
On a sudden as I faced it,
The garment seemed to me like a mirror of myself.
I saw it all in my whole self,
Moreover I faced my whole self in facing it.
For we were two in distinction,
And yet again one in one likeness.
And the treasurers also,
Who brought it to me, I saw in like manner,
That they were twain yet one likeness.
For one kingly sign was graven on them,
Of *his* hands that restored to me
My treasure and my wealth by means of them.
My bright embroidered robe,
Which . . . with glorious colours;
With gold and with beryls,
And rubies and agates
And sardonyxes varied in colour,
It also was made ready in its home on high
And with stones of adamant
All its seams were fastened;
And the image of the King of kings was depicted in full all over it,
And like the sapphire stone also were its manifold hues.
Again I saw that all over it
The motions of knowledge were stirring
And as if to speak
I saw it also making itself ready.
I heard the sound of its tones,
Which it uttered to those who brought it down

.   .   .   .

Saying 'I am the active in deeds.'
And I also perceived in myself
That my stature was growing according to his labours.
And in its kingly motions
It poured itself entirely over me
And in the hands of its givers
It hastened that I might take it.
And me too my love urged on

That I should run to meet it and receive it;
And I stretched forth and received it,
With the beauty of its colours I adorned myself
And my toga of brilliant colours
I cast around me, in its whole breadth.
I clothed myself therewith, and ascended
To the gate of salutation and homage;
I bowed my head, and did homage
To the Majesty of my Father who had sent it to me,
For I had done his commandments,
And he too had done what he promised,
And at the gate of his princes
I mingled with his nobles;
For he rejoiced in me and received me,
And I was with him in his kingdom.
And with the voice . . .
All his servants glorify him.
And he promised that also to the gate
Of the King of kings I should speed with him,
And bringing my gift and my pearl
I should appear with him before our King.

BIBLIOGRAPHY

ANANDA COOMARASWAMY – Hinduism and Buddhism, *Philosophical Library, New York*.
The Dance of Shiva, *Asia Publishing House, Bombay*
GERALDINE COSTER – Yoga and Western Psychology, *O.U.P.*
THE LAMA KAZI DAWA-SANDUP AND DR W. Y. EVANS-WENTZ – The Tibetan Book of the Dead, *O.U.P.*
Tibetan Yoga and Secret Doctrine, *O.U.P.*
Tibet's Great Yoga Milarepa, *O.U.P.*
THE LAMA ANAGARIKA GOVINDA – Foundations of Tibetan Mysticism, *Rider*
EDMOND HOLMES – The Creed of Buddha, *The Bodley Head*
C. G. JUNG – Psychology and Religion, *Yale University Press*
The Undiscovered Self, *Routledge and Kegan Paul*
Flying Saucers: A Modern Myth of Things Seen in the Skies, *Routledge and Kegan Paul*
The Secret of the Golden Flower (Richard Wilhelm and C. G. Jung), *Routledge and Kegan Paul*
G. R. S. MEAD – Fragments of a Faith Forgotten, *Watkins*
Thrice Greatest Hermes, *Watkins*
G. H. MEES – The Revelation in the Wilderness, Vols I-III, *N. Kluwer-Deventer*
MAURICE NICOLL – The Mark, *Vincent Stuart*
The New Man, *Vincent Stuart*
SRI KRISHNA PREM – The Yoga of the Bhagavad Gita, *Watkins*
The Yoga of the Kathopanishad, *Watkins*
D. T. SUZUKI – An Introduction to Zen Buddhism, *Rider*
Essays in Zen Buddhism, *Rider*
Mysticism – Christian and Buddhist, *George Allen and Unwin*
ALAN WATTS – Myth and Ritual in Christianity, *Thames and Hudson*
HEINRICH ZIMMER – The Art of Indian Asia, *Bollingen Series, Pantheon*
The King and the Corpse, *Bollingen Series, Pantheon*

Angkor

G. COEDES – Pour mieux comprendre Angkor, *Maisonneuve, Paris* 1947
G. DE CORAL-REMUSAT – L'Art Khmer; les grandes étapes de son évolution, *Editions d'Art et d'Histoire, Paris* 1940
B. PH. GROSLIER – Angkor, *Arthaud*
G. GROSLIER – Recherches sur les Cambodgiens, *Challamel, Paris* 1921
G. T. HALL – A History of South-East Asia, *Macmillan*
P. LOTI – Un Pelerin d'Angkor, *Calmann-Levy, Paris* 1912
M. MACDONALD – Angkor, *Macmillan*
O. SITWELL – Escape with me, *Macmillan*

Miniature Painting

W. G. ARCHER – Indian Painting, *Batsford*
Kangra Painting, *Faber*
The Loves of Krishna, *Allen and Unwin*

Bali

M. COVARRUBIAS – Island of Bali, *New York* 1937

BASIL GRAY – Buddhist Cave Paintings at Tun-Huang, *Faber*